培梅家常菜

銷售20萬冊紀念版

作者簡介
About the Author

傅培梅 老師

自1955年即開始開班授課，致力於發揚中國飲食文化。1962年開始擔任電視烹飪教學之節目至今，示範無數美味之菜點。亦經常應邀或奉派赴世界各國做特別表演和講習，獲得好評，更因表現優異、貢獻良多而得到多項頒獎與表揚。同時亦致力於食品加工之研究，以期使中國美食走向現代化，深入每一個家庭。

著有中、英、日文食譜五十餘本，銷售海內外各地，藉而推廣與發揚中華美饌。

Fu Pel Mei is the most famous and distinguished culinary artist in Taiwan In1955, she established "Pei Mei's Chinese cooking Institute of Taipei". She also started a weekly cooking demonstration program, "Fu Pei Mei's Time", on T.T.V.Co.(Taiwan) in 1962, and the show still airs today.

Fu Pel Mei has been a recognized recipient of numberous awards for her tremendous contribution to the awareness and understanding of Chinese traditions and culture.

Pei Mei has written more then 50 cook books which include Chinese, English and Japanese versions.

程安琪 老師

大學畢業後即跟隨母親學習烹飪，已有26年烹飪教學經驗，主持許多電視教學節目，現在與母親主持台視"傅培梅時間"，親切認真的教學、仔細的解說受到許多觀眾喜愛。現任教於台北市農會。

著作有：美味台菜、精緻家常菜、創意家常菜、輕鬆上菜系列、廚房講義、一網打盡百味魚、熱炒、動手做醃菜等四十餘本食譜書。

Under the guidance of her mother Pei Mei, Angela learned many principles and techniques of Chinese cooking and has herself become an expert chef. She has 26 years of experience in teaching Chinese cooking,and is a very popular cooking instructor now. She also has many TV program for cooking demonstration.

Angela has written more than 40 cook books, including works such as "Gourmet Cooking1-4","Fish 100","Easy Stir-frying".

貼心
Only for you

　　距離1984年母親出版"培梅家常菜"至今，已經19年了，這本累積銷售超過60萬冊的食譜，在母親眾多出版品中，一直是最受讀者喜歡的廚房寶典，誠如母親所說："家常菜即是家庭中日常烹飪之菜餚，製作方法應力求簡單，配料、佐料之種類不可繁雜，採用之主要材料，也以經濟、實惠為主"，而且"家常菜既屬家庭日常烹飪者，故不需苛求外觀，尤其是餐盤之點綴、裝飾皆可省略，但其他條件，如口味、營養價值等，則必須講求、不宜疏忽。為了增進家人的食慾和健康，家常菜也應在口味上和烹調技術方法上力求變化"。這些烹飪心得，歷經20年，仍然是各位讀者在為家人準備可口佳餚時，所應了解的。

　　飲食習慣隨著時代的進步不斷改變，閱讀的視覺享受，也隨著科技的進步而要求愈高，為了傳承母親這本膾炙人口的食譜，大姊安琪和我決定替母親重新製作她這本經典代表作"培梅家常菜"，經母親和大姊仔細的選題，重新研究調味下，在大姊掌廚，媽媽學生陳盈舟老師幫助下，辛苦工作了無數個日夜，終於完成了新版"培梅家常菜"的拍攝工作，我們並特別邀請了最注重出版品質的躍昇文化公司總經理林蔚穎先生，為本書完成後製工作，希望給讀者帶來另一份驚喜。

　　It's been 19 years since Pei Mei's Homestyle Cooking was first published in 1984, This cookbook has sold more Than six hundred thousand copies and has become one of the most popular "must -have's " for every kitchen. Just as my mom said, "homestyle cooking is meant for everday family meals. The methods should be simplistic, made with common economical ingredients. In fact, since the meals are to be enjoyed by the family omamentation can be omitted. However, the tastes, nutrirional values, and other important qualities should not be neglected and are enhanced by variations in cooking techniqes. "The culinary wisdom contained in this volume has been around for 20 years and should be known to the readers while preparing home cooked meals for the family .

　　Just as eating habits have changed with time, the demand for improved quality of cookbooks has increased. To carry on the most popular of my mother's cookbooks, my sister Angela and I decided to completely remark Pei Mei Homestyle Cooking. After testing and revising certain ingredients, my mother and sister carefully selected to recreate recipes to bring out the most delicious dishes. Through many days of hard work with my sister and mother's studenet, Miss Cheng Ying Zhou, we finaly finished the photography for Pei Mei's Homestyle Cooking . We also specially invited Mr. Ling Wei Ying from Culture & Life Publishing Co. to finish the publishing of book. We hope to bring to you one more pleasant surprise.

目 錄
Contents

作者介紹 2
貼心 3

豬肉類 Pork

東坡肉 8
Stewed Pork with Brown Sauce

回鍋肉 9
Double Cooked Pork

咕咾肉 10
Sweet & Sour Pork

炒木須肉 11
Mo-shu Pork

粉蒸小排骨 12
Steamed Spareribs with Rice Powder

梅乾菜燒肉 13
Stewed Pork with Fermented Cabbage

酥炸大排骨 14
Deep-fried Pork Steak

豉椒炒排骨 15
Spareribs with Fermented Black Beans

紅燒百頁捲 16
Stewed Bean Curd Rolls

洋蔥燴豬排 18
Pork Steak, Western Style

南煎肉丸子 19
Pork Hamburgers, Home-Style

鹹蛋蒸肉餅 20
Steamed Pork with Salted Eggs

燒滷豬腳 21
Stewed Pork Feet

家常獅子頭 22
Stewed Lion's Head

糖醋豬小排 24
Sweet & Sour Spareribs

螞蟻上樹 25
Minced Pork with Bean Threads

魚香蹄花 26
Stewed Pork Feet with Hot Sauce

爆炒豬肝 27
Quick Stir-fried Pork Liver

雞鴨類 Chicken and Duck

梅醬雞 28
Chicken with Plum Sauce

棒棒雞 30
Bon Bon Chicken

三杯雞 31
Three Cups Chicken

五香滷雞 32
Braised Chicken with Spicy Brown Sauce

琥珀雞凍 34
Jellied Chicken

左公雞 36
Stir-fried Chicken-Hunan Style

紅燒雞 37
Stewed Chicken, with Brown Sauce

銀芽雞絲 38
Stir-fried Chicken Shreds

鹽酥雞塊 39
Deep-fried Crispy Chicken

醬爆雞丁 40
Chicken with Sweet Soy Bean Paste

香酥雞腿 41
Crispy Chicken Legs

蔥油淋雞腿 42
Steamed Chicken with Green Onion Sauce
豉汁蒸雞球 43
Chicken with Fermented Black Beans
金針雲耳雞 44
Stewed Chicken, Country Style
八寶封雞腿 46
Steamed Chicken Pudding
冬菜鴨 47
Steamed Duck with Salted Cabbage
什錦扒肥鴨 48
Stewed Duck with Assorted Vegetables
芹菜拌鴨條 50
Roasted Duck Salad
胡蔥鴨 51
Stewed Duck with Scallion
燴鴨絲羹 52
Duck Potage

牛羊類

袈裟牛肉 53
Deep-fried Beef Sandwich
五彩牛柳 54
Five - Colored Beef Strips
麻辣牛肉 56
Sliced Beef with Chili Sauce
白灼牛肉片 57
Poached Beef Slices, Hong Kong Style
咖哩燒牛腩 58
Braised Beef with Curry Sauce
蔥薑焗牛肉 59
Beef with Green Onion and Ginger
漢堡牛肉餅 60
Home Style Hamburgers
鮮茄牛腩 62
Stewed Beef with Tomato
蔥爆羊肉 63
Sautéed Lamb with Scallion
砂鍋羊肉 64
Stewed Lamb in Casserole Dish

海鮮類

脆底蝦仁 66
Stir-fried Shrimp with Yu-tiau
茄汁蝦仁 68
Stir-fried Shrimp with Ketchup
蒜蓉蒸草蝦 69
Steamed Prawns with Garlic Sauce
乾燒明蝦段 70
Sautéed Prawns with Hot Sauce

目錄

碧綠琵琶蝦 72
Steamed Prawns

西蘭鳳尾蝦 74
Stir-fried Prawns with Broccoli

生炒蝦鬆 76
Stir-fried Minced Shrimp

炒蔭豉蚵 78
Stir-fried Oysters

蔥薑焗鮮蟹 79
Braised Crabs with Green Onion

家常魷魚捲 80
Stir-fried Squid Rolls with Chili Sauce

宮保蟹腿肉 81
Crab Legs Gung-Bao Sauce

八寶鑲鮮魷 82
Stuffed Squid

三鮮鍋巴 84
Popped Rice with Seafood Sauce

酸辣海參 86
Shredded Sea Cucumber with Minced Pork

墨魚大燒 88
Stewed Cuttlefish with Pork

魚類

蔥燒鯽魚 89
Braised Fish with Green Onion

辣豆瓣魚 90
Carp with Hot Bean Sauce

豆酥鯧魚 92
Steamed Fish with Yellow Bean Sauce

乾燒帶魚 91
Braised Fish with Brown Sauce

西湖醋魚 94
West Lake Fish

大蒜黃魚 96
Stewed Yellow Croaker with Garlic

雙味魚捲 97
Two Flavored Fish Rolls

蠔油魚片 98
Fish Fillet with Oyster Sauce

酥炸魚條 99
Deep-fried Crispy Fish

廣式清蒸魚 100
Steamed Fish, Cantonese Style

糖醋溜全魚 101
Sweet & Sour Fish

乾燒大魚頭 102
Stewed Fish Head

蛋、豆腐類

琵琶豆腐 103
Pipa Shaped Bean Curd Balls

麻婆豆腐 104
Ma Po's Bean Curd

紅燒豆腐 105
Braised Bean Curd with Ham

炒豆乾絲 106
Stir-fried Bean Curd Strings

蝦仁豆腐 107
Bean Curd with Shrimp

脆皮炸豆腐 108
Crispy Bean Curd

燒豆腐包 109
Stewed Bean Curd Package

三鮮烘蛋 110
Omelet, Chinese Style
蕃茄炒蛋 112
Stir-fried Eggs with Tomato
碎肉蒸蛋 113
Steamed Eggs with Minced Pork
麵拖老蛋 114
Deep-fried Boiled Egg with Clear Sauce
紅燒蛋餃 115
Stewed Egg Dumplings with Vegetable

蔬菜類
糖醋蓮白捲 116
Sweet & Sour Cabbage Rolls
酸辣黃瓜 118
Hot & Sour Cucumbers
拌海蜇皮 119
Jellyfish Salad
芥末拌洋芹 120
Celery Salad with Mustard
炒肉絲拉皮 121
Stir-fried Pork Salad
魚香溜茄夾 122
Stuffed Eggplants, Sze-chuan Style
肉末四季豆 123
String Beans with Pork
雪菜炒肉絲 124
stir-fried Pork with Mustard Green
素炒十香菜 125
Stir-fired Assorted Vegetables
干貝鮮筍衣 126
Slice Bamboo Shoots with Dried Scallop
醬燒茄子 127
Eggplants with Sweet Soybean Paste

醋烹銀芽 128
Quick Stir-fried Bean Sprouts
三絲空心菜 129
Stir-fried Water Convolvalus
五味苦瓜 130
Bitter Gourd with Rich Sauce
酥肉蒸蘿蔔 131
Steamed Pork with Radish

湯類
腰片湯 132
Sliced Kidney Sonp
酸辣湯 133
Hot & Sour Soup
連鍋湯 134
Sticed Pork Soup, Sze-chuan Style
蝦丸湯 135
Shrimp Ball Soup
鳳梨苦瓜雞 136
Chicken Soup with Pineapple
香菇肉羹 138
Meat Potage
冬菇燉雞湯 139
Chicken & Black Mushroom Soup
排骨蔬菜湯 140
Sparerib & Vegetable Soup
蟹肉豆腐羹 142
Crab Meat Potage
蘿蔔絲蛤蜊湯 143
Clams & Radish Soup

【附錄】
烹飪入門光碟食譜 144

豬肉類

東坡肉
Stewed Pork with Brown Sauce

材料：
豬五花肉1斤、蔥5支、薑2片、八角2顆、草繩或棉繩4條、青菜適量

調味料：
糖2大匙、酒1/2杯、醬油2/3杯

做法：
1. 五花肉連皮洗淨，放鍋內用滾水煮30分鐘（酌加蔥、薑），切成5公分四方大小，用草繩或棉繩綁好。
2. 在炒鍋內燒熱2大匙油後，煸炒白糖成茶黃色，待起大泡時，加入醬油、酒及煮肉之湯汁，再放下蔥、薑、八角與肉塊，用小火再燒煮30分鐘（肉皮應向上放，以免黏住鍋底）。
3. 將肉塊夾到小瓷罐或深口碗中，注入湯汁，用保鮮膜封住口，上鍋蒸2小時以上至肉塊十分酥爛。
4. 湯汁以大火收濃稠些，淋在肉上，配炒青菜上桌。

   * 此菜另一種燒法是直接用小火煮2小時至肉極爛為止。

   * **You may continue to stew the pork in the wok for 2 hours until very tender.**

Ingredients：
600. pork belly with skin, any green vegetable, 5stalks green onion, 2slices ginger, 2 star anise, 4 strings

Seasonings：
2T. sugar, 1/2 C. wine, 2/3 C. soy sauce

Procedures：
1. Clean the pork, place in a pot; add 1 green onion, 1 slice ginger and 2 C. of water, cook for 1/2 hour. Cut the pork into 4 pieces about 5cm square. Tie with the strings.
2. Heat 2T. oil to stir-fry sugar over low heat until the sugar becomes light brown and bubbles. Add soy sauce, wine, and soup from cooked pork. Add green onion, ginger, star anise and pork. Stew for another half hour (place the skin side up, so the pork will not stick to the wok).
3. Remove the pork and place in a large bowl. Add the liquid; seal andsteam for 2 hours until very tender.
4. pour the liquid to a pot, thicken it over high heat, pour over pork, serve with stir-fried vegetable.

回鍋肉
Double Cooked Pork

材料：

豬肉（五花肉或後腿肉）6兩、高麗菜半斤、豆腐乾5塊、紅辣椒2支、青蒜1支

調味料：

甜麵醬2大匙、醬油1大匙、水1大匙、辣豆瓣醬1/2大匙、糖2茶匙

做法：

1. 豬肉要選購約有4公分寬度的一整塊，洗淨後放入水中（加酒和蔥、薑），煮約30分鐘左右，至已熟透（可用筷子由肉中間插入，如無血水滲出且能輕易插透，便是已熟），撈出後待冷，逆紋切成大薄片。
2. 高麗菜洗淨後，切成4公分大小之塊狀；豆腐乾斜刀片成薄片；紅辣椒去籽切丁；青蒜切絲備用。
3. 甜麵醬放在小碗內加入調味料調勻備用。
4. 鍋內燒熱2大匙油，將肉片放入，爆炒至肥肉部分的油已滲出，瘦肉呈捲曲狀，將肉盛出。用餘油來炒高麗菜及豆腐乾，加少許清水將高麗菜炒軟亦盛出。
5. 另用1大匙油炒香甜麵醬料，至有香氣時，才將肉片等倒回鍋內炒勻，放下紅辣椒及青蒜便可盛出。

Ingredients:

250g. pork (bacon or leg part), 300g. cabbage, 5 pieces dried bean curd, 2 red chilies, 1 green garlic

Seasonings：

2T. sweet soybean paste, 1T. soy sauce, 1T. water, 1/2T. hot bean paste, 2t. sugar

Procedures：

1. Boil the pork with a little wine, ginger and green onion for about 30 minutes, remove. After cools, cut into very thin slices.
2. Cut the cabbage into 4cm pieces；slice the dried bean curd；remove the seeds from the red chilies and dice；shred the green garlic.
3. Mix the sweet bean paste with other seasonings in a bowl.
4. Fry the pork slices with 2T. oil for 1 minute. Remove the pork. Stir-fry cabbage and dried bean curd with the remaining oil, add a little water, cook until the cabbage becomes soft. Remove.
5. Use another 1T. oil to stir-fry the sauce for 15 seconds. Return the pork and cabbage to the wok, mixing thoroughly. Add red chilies and green garlic. Serve.

咕咾肉
Sweet & Sour Pork

材料：
豬大排骨肉（或夾心肉）半斤、青椒1個、酸果1杯、鳳梨2片、太白粉1杯

調味料：
（1）醬油1大匙、蛋黃1個、太白粉1大匙、水1大匙
（2）番茄醬3大匙、糖3大匙、醋3大匙、水6大匙、鹽1/4茶匙、麻油1/2茶匙、太白粉2茶匙

做法：
1. 將大排骨肉橫面剖開成一大片，用刀背來回將肉拍鬆，再切成2公分大小，用調味料（1）拌醃半小時。
2. 青椒去籽、切小塊；鳳梨每片切成八小塊。
3. 在一碗內先調好調味料（2）備用。
4. 肉塊沾上太白粉，投入熱油中，大火炸至金黃而熟時撈出。油再燒熱，將肉塊再炸約10秒鐘，撈出。
5. 另燒熱2大匙油，爆香青椒及酸果、鳳梨塊，然後倒下調味料（2），用大火煮滾，馬上熄火。將炸好的肉塊落鍋，快速翻炒數下，即可裝盤。

* "酸果"即廣東泡菜，係用白蘿蔔、胡蘿蔔、小黃瓜等切小滾刀塊，用鹽醃2小時後擠乾，泡入糖醋汁（糖、白醋、冷開水各1/2杯）中約2～3小時即可取食。

Ingredients：
300g. pork tenderloin, 1 green pepper, 4 slices pineapple, 1C. Cantonese pickles, 1C. cornstarch

Seasonings：
（1）1T. soy sauce, 1 egg yolk, 1T. cornstarch, 1T. water
（2）3T. ketchup, 3T. sugar, 3T. white vinegar, 6T. water, 1/4t. salt, 1/2t.. sesame oil, 2t. cornstarch

Procedures:
1. Pound pork with the back of a cleaver (this is to tenderize the pork), then cut into 1" cubes. Marinate for at least 1/2 hour.
2. Remove seeds from green pepper, cut into 1" squares；cut the pineapple into 8 small pieces per slice.
3. Mix the seasoning (2) in s small bowl.
4. Coat the pork with cornstarch. Deep-fry in hot oil over high heat until done. Remove the pork. Reheat the oil and deep-fry again until crispy. Remove pork.
5. In 2T. oil, stir-fry green pepper, pickles and pineapple. Add seasoning sauce, bring to a boil, turn off heat. Add pork. Mix well and serve immediately.

* Cantonese pickles：Cut radish, carrots and small cucumber into cube. Soak with salt for 2 hours. Rinse and squeeze out excess moisture. Soak in sweet and sour juice (1/2 C. sugar, 1/2 C. white vinegar, and 1/2 C. water) for another 2~3 hours.

炒木須肉
Mo-shu Pork

材料：
豬前腿肉4兩、水發木耳半杯、蛋2個、菠菜3兩、筍1支、蔥花1大匙

調味料：
（1） 醬油½大匙、太白粉½大匙、水1大匙
（2） 醬油1大匙、鹽¼茶匙

做法：

1. 豬肉切絲後，用調味料（1）拌勻，醃上10分鐘左右。
2. 菠菜切成3公分長段；筍煮熟後切絲；蛋加¼茶匙鹽打散後，先用少許油炒熟。
3. 將油½杯燒熱至八分熱，落肉絲下鍋過油，待變色即撈出、瀝乾。
4. 僅留下2大匙油，先將蔥花放入爆香，再加入筍絲、木耳絲及菠菜炒熟，再放下已炒熟之肉絲及蛋，並加醬油和鹽調味，大火鏟拌均勻便可盛出裝盤。

＊ 木須肉食用時多配上蔥段、甜麵醬及薄餅上桌包食。

＊ **Usually this dish is served with green onion (cut into 5cm sections), sweet soy bean paste, and spring roll skins.**

Ingredients：
150g. lean pork, ½C. shredded black wood ear, 2 eggs, 120g. spinach, 1 bamboo shoot, 1T. chopped green onion

Seasonings：
（1） ½T. soy sauce, ½T. cornstarch, 1T. water
（2） 1T. soy sauce, ¼t. salt

Procedures:

1. Shred the pork. Marinate with seasonings (1) for 10 minutes.
2. Trim and cut the spinach into sections 3cm long；cook and shred the bamboo shoot； beat the eggs with ¼ t. salt, stir-fry quickly so the pieces will be small.
3. Heat ½C. oil to 160°C, stir-fry the pork until done, remove.
4. Use only 2T. oil to stir-fry green onions. Add the bamboo shoot, black wood ear, and spinach stir-fry for 30 seconds. Add the pork and egg. Season with soy sauce, salt. Mix thoroughly over high heat. Remove and serve.

粉蒸小排骨
Steamed Spareribs with Rice Powder

材料：
小排骨半斤、蕃薯6兩、蒸肉粉1杯、蔥屑1大匙

調味料：
淡色醬油2大匙、酒1大匙、糖1/2茶匙、甜麵醬1/2大匙、
辣豆瓣醬1/2大匙、油2大匙、水2大匙、
胡椒粉1/4茶匙

做法：

1. 調味料拌勻，醃半小時左右。
  將蒸肉粉倒入小排骨中，再仔細拌勻，使每塊均沾上
2. 蒸肉粉，排在中型麵碗或鋁盤中。
3. 蕃薯去皮切滾刀塊，放在排骨上，大火蒸1小時以上。
4. 將碗倒扣在盤中，使粉蒸排骨扣出，撒下蔥花，淋上
  少許熱油，趁熱上桌。

  ＊ 如果家中有竹製小蒸籠，可裝在蒸籠中蒸，則風味更佳。
  ＊ 蒸肉粉是將在來米70%加糯米30%混合，加入八角、花椒等同炒至微黃而透香氣，冷後研磨成粗粉狀便是。

  ＊ **If you have a small bamboo steamer, you may use it to steam this dish.**

＊ **Flavored rice powder is 70% ordinary rice and 30% glutinous rice, stir-fry with star anise and brown peppercorn until the rice becomes yellowish-brown, cooled and mashed into a powder.**

Ingredients：
300g. pork spareribs, 250g. sweet potato,
1C. flavored rice powder, 1T. chopped green onion

Seasonings：
2T. light color soy sauce, 1T. wine, 1/2t. sugar,
1/2T. sweet soy bean paste, 1/2T. hot bean paste, 2T. oil,
2T. water, 1/4 t. black pepper

Procedures:

1. Cut the spareribs into pieces 2cm long. Put into a bowl and marinate with the seasonings for 1/2 hour.
2. Add the flavored rice powder in, mix with spareribs thoroughly. Arrange in a steaming bowl.
3. Peel sweet potatoes, cut into 1" cubes and place on top of spareribs. Steam over high heat for about 1 hours.
4. Turn the bowl over onto a platter to remove the spareribs. Sprinkle chopped green onion over the spareribs and then pour 1T. heated oil over the green onions. Serve hot.

梅乾菜燒肉

Stewed Pork with Fermented Cabbage

材料：
豬五花肉12兩、蔥2支、薑2片、梅乾菜1兩（約1杯）

調味料：
醬油3大匙、酒1大匙、糖1大匙、八角1顆、開水3杯

做法：

1. 將豬肉連皮切成2公分寬之塊狀，用醬油泡10分鐘，再投入熱油中炸黃。
2. 另用2大匙油煎香蔥段及薑片，然後淋下酒、泡肉所剩餘之醬油、糖及八角，並放下肉塊，用大火炒拌數下後即注入開水，改用小火燒煮半小時左右。
3. 梅乾菜泡在水中，拌洗乾淨後切碎並再擠乾，放入第二項之肉中繼續用小火同燒半小時，至肉夠爛為止。

* 此菜也可在加入梅乾菜後，盛入碗內，上鍋蒸30分鐘至菜和肉夠爛。

* You may steam the pork after adding the fermented cabbage, steam until the pork is tender enough.

* If you don't have fermented cabbage, you may just stew pork with this way.

Ingredients：
450g. pork belly with skin, 2stalks green onion, 2slices ginger, 40g. fermented cabbage (about 1 cup)

Seasonings：
3T. soy sauce, 1T. wine, 1T. sugar, 1star-anise, 3C. boiling water

Procedures：

1. Cut the pork into pieces 2cm×3cm Soak with soy sauce for 10 minutes. Deep-fry with hot oil for 20 seconds.
2. Fry green onion sections and ginger with 2T. oil. Sprinkle with wine, soy sauce (remained from marinating the pork), sugar, and star anise. Add pork, stir-fry over high heat for about 1 minute. Add water and simmer for $1/2$ hour.
3. Soak the fermented cabbage in water. Clean and chop, squeeze and add to the pork. Simmer for another $1/2$ hour until the pork is tender.

酥炸大排骨
Deep-fried Pork Steak

材料：
大排骨肉4片、蔥1支、薑2片、蕃薯粉4大匙、麵粉2大匙

調味料：
酒1/2大匙、醬油2大匙、糖2茶匙、水2大匙、胡椒粉1/2茶匙

做法：

1. 大排骨肉選購帶花的部分（肉質較嫩），洗淨後用刀背搥敲，使肉變大、同時使肉質鬆軟。
2. 在大碗中，將醃肉料（包括調味料及拍過之蔥、薑）調勻，肉片放進拌好，醃20分鐘以上。
3. 在大碗中將蕃薯粉及麵粉混合，沾裹在大排骨上。鍋中燒熱炸油，將排骨一片片投下去炸，約炸2分鐘後，將排骨撈出，將油再燒熱一次，重將肉片再用大火炸酥（約30秒鐘）便可撈出、瀝乾油汁。

Ingredients：
4 pieces pork steak, 1stalk green onion, 2 slices ginger, 4T. sweet potato powder, 2T. flour

Seasonings：
1/2T. wine, 2T. soy sauce, 2T. sugar, 2T. water, 1/2t. pepper

Procedures：

1. Choose the tender part of the pork steak. Rinse and pound each slice with back of cleaver to tenderize it.
2. In a large bowl, mix the seasonings with crushed green onion, and ginger together. Marinate pork for about 20 minutes.
3. Mix sweet potato powder and flour together; coat the pork. Deep-fry in hot oil for 2 minutes. Remove the pork. Reheat the oil, deep-fry the pork again (about 30 seconds). Remove the pork. Drain off the oil.

* 炸排骨的口味有許多種，有醃後不裹粉的乾炸和裹乾麵粉或麵包粉或蕃薯粉的酥炸；以及調成麵糊裹住的軟炸等方式，可隨個人喜好炸之。

* **There are many ways to deep-fry pork steak. This is the Taiwanese method. You may just deep-fry the pork without any coating, or coat with only flour or bread crumbs or sweet potato powder, or you may mix a flour paste to coat the pork.**

豉椒炒排骨
Spareribs with Fermented Black Beans

材料：
小排骨半斤、青椒1個、紅辣椒2支、大蒜片2大匙、蔥段2大匙、豆豉2大匙

調味料：
（1）醬油1大匙、太白粉1大匙
（2）酒1/2大匙、醬油1大匙、水1杯、鹽1/4茶匙、糖1茶匙

做法：
1. 小排骨斬切成1公分寬、2公分長之小塊，用調味料（1）拌醃10分鐘。
2. 青、紅辣椒去籽後，切成1公分四方大小；豆豉用冷水泡5分鐘後略切；蔥切斜段。
3. 鍋中燒熱3大匙油，將小排骨落鍋大火拌炒至肉變白色後，放下豆豉、大蒜及蔥段，繼續拌炒，並淋下酒、醬油及水，燜煮3分鐘。
4. 加入青、紅辣椒並放鹽、糖調味，以大火收乾湯汁，即可裝盤。

Ingredients：
300g. spareribs, 1 green pepper, 2 red chilies, 2T. sliced garlic, 2T. green onion sections, 2T. fermented black beans

Seasonings：
（1） 1T. wine, 1T. corn starch
（2） 1/2T. wine, 1T. soy sauce, 1C. water, 1/2t. salt, 1t. sugar

Procedures:
1. Cut the spareribs into 1cm×2cm pieces. marinate with seasonings (1) for 10 minutes.
2. Remove the seeds from the green pepper and red chilies, cut into 1cm squares；soak the fermented black beans for 5 minutes.
3. Heat 3T. oil to stir-fry spareribs until the meat turns light. Add garlic, fermented black beans, and green onion, stir-fry continually. Add wine, soy sauce, and water; cook over low heat for 3 minutes.
4. Add green pepper and red chili, season with salt and sugar. Cook over high heat until the liquid is absorbed. Remove to plate and serve.

豬肉類

16

紅燒百頁捲
Stewed Bean Curd Rolls

材料：
絞肉6兩、百頁10張、蔥屑1大匙、青江菜8棵、小蘇打粉1/2茶匙

調味料：
（1）醬油1茶匙、鹽1/3茶匙、麻油1茶匙、水2大匙
（2）醬油1大匙、水1/4杯、糖1/2茶匙

做法：

1. 在5杯開水中將小蘇打粉溶化，放入10張百頁浸泡。見百頁顏色變白且變軟時，便可將百頁取出，放在清水中漂洗，此時因百頁已夠軟，小心取出。
2. 絞肉再加以剁爛後，放下調味料（1），用筷子朝同一方向攪拌均勻。
3. 取一張百頁，將十分之一的肉餡放在百頁上，包捲成6~7公分長的筒狀。全部做好，放在一個盤子中，上鍋蒸10分鐘，使百頁捲定型，不致散開。
4. 蒸過之百頁捲連湯汁倒在鍋中，再加水、醬油、糖，以小火燒10分鐘左右，盛入盤中，再附上炒過之青江菜。

Ingredients：
250g. ground pork, 10 pieces bean curd sheet, 1T. chopped green onion, 8 stalks green cabbage, 1/2t. baking soda

Seasonings：
（1）1t. soy sauce, 1/3t. salt, 2T. water, 1t. sesame oil
（2）1T. soy sauce, 1/4C. water, 1t. sugar

Procedures：

1. Mix 1/2t. baking soda in 5C. of boiling water to soak the bean curd sheets until the sheets turn white and become soft, rinse with water.
2. Chop the ground pork again. Place in a large bowl. Add green onion and seasonings (1). Stir in the same direction for one minute.
3. Place 1/10 of the meat mixture on one piece of bean curd sheet. Roll and fold to make a roll about 6~7cm long (like a spring roll). Place on a plate, and continue to make the other rolls. Steam for 10 minutes to make the shape firm.
4. Pour the rolls and liquid into a wok. Add seasonings (2). Cook over low heat for 10 minutes. Remove to the serving plate, serve with the stir-fried green cabbage.

*百頁捲亦可不用紅燒，直接蒸20分鐘左右，蒸時將醬油1大匙淋在百頁捲上便可。
*You may steam the rolls for 20 minutes until done, pour 1T. soy sauce over rolls beforesteam it.
*You may use thin egg pancake sheets instead of bean curd sheets.

洋蔥燴豬排
Pork Steak, Western Style

材料：
大排骨肉4片、洋蔥1個、胡蘿蔔半支、洋菇10粒、麵粉1/2杯

調味料：
（1）鹽1茶匙、胡椒粉1/4茶匙、酒1/2大匙
（2）番茄醬或番茄膏3大匙、鹽1/3茶匙、糖1茶匙、水2杯

做法：
1. 用刀面拍打大排骨肉，使肉質變鬆而肉片伸大，然後撒上調味料（1），醃約15分鐘。
2. 洋蔥、胡蘿蔔分別切細絲；洋菇切片。
3. 將醃好的大排骨肉兩面各沾裹麵粉，一片片放入熱油中，煎至表面呈黃褐色，盛出後，將油倒出。
4. 另用2大匙油炒洋蔥、胡蘿蔔和洋菇，以中火慢慢將洋蔥炒軟且有香味透出。放下調味料（2），和豬排，一起用中火煮15分鐘，中途要翻動一、兩次。
5. 如湯汁還有很多，可用大火收乾，裝盤上桌。

   ＊因豬排沾有麵粉，煮過後湯汁自然成濃稠狀。如果喜歡用湯汁拌飯，則水可增加1杯。肉也可切成小塊裝盤。

Ingredients：
4 pork steaks, 1 onion, 1/2 carrot, 10 mushrooms, 1/2C. flour

Seasonings：
（1）1 t. salt, 1/4t. black pepper, 1/2T. wine
（2）3T. tomato paste or ketchup, 1/3t. salt, 1t. sugar, 2C. water

Procedures:
1. Rinse and pat the pork dry. Pound with the back of the cleaver to tenderize, marinate with seasonings (10) for 15 minutes.
2. Shred the onion and carrot；slice the mushrooms.
3. Coat the pork with flour. Fry with hot oil piece by piece. When the color turns light brown, remove.
4. Stir-fry vegetable with 2T. oil over medium heat until the onion is soft. Add seasonings (2) and pork, cook for 15 minutes over medium heat (stir once or twice to keep the mixture from sticking to the wok).
5. If there is too much sauce left, you may use high heat to reduce it.

   ＊**This dish is good served over rice, you may add 1C. water more to get enough sauce for rice. Cut the pork smaller, if you wish.**

南煎肉丸子
Pork Hamburgers, Home-Style

材料：
豬絞肉半斤、小芥藍菜8支、薑絲1大匙、蔥絲2大匙

調味料：
（1）蛋1個、薑末1茶匙、蔥屑1大匙、酒1/2大匙、
　　 鹽1/4茶匙、醬油1/2大匙、太白粉1大匙、麵粉1大匙
（2）酒1/2大匙、醬油2大匙、水1杯、太白粉1/2大匙、
　　 麻油少許

做法：
1. 將買回來的絞肉再仔細剁過，使肉增加彈性。放在盆中，加入調味料（1），用五、六支筷子、朝同一方向攪拌，使肉更有黏性。
2. 在熱鍋內放1/2杯油，將鍋子端起搖動一下，使鍋底四周沾油。將火熄掉，把肉做成8個丸子放入鍋中，並用鏟子沾油，把每一個丸子壓扁一點，成為直徑3公分左右，再開火煎黃丸子（一面煎好後再翻面煎）。
3. 撒下薑絲，淋下酒和醬油，加水、蓋上鍋蓋，用小火煮5分鐘。
4. 淋下少許太白粉水勾芡，使湯汁變稠，再撒下蔥絲、淋下麻油，裝入盤中，周圍用炒過之芥藍菜（加鹽調味）圍邊。

Ingredients：
300g. ground pork, 8 stalks green vegetable,
1T. shredded ginger, 2T. shredded green onion

Seasonings：
(1) 1 egg, 1t. smashed ginger, 1T. chopped green onion,
　　 1/2T. wine, 1/2t. salt, 1T. soy sauce, 1T. cornstarch,
　　 1T. flour
(2) 1/2T. wine, 2T. soy sauce, 1C. water,
　　 1/2T. cornstarch paste, 1/4t. sesame oil

Procedures：
1. Chop the ground pork again to make the pork finer and stickier. Mix with the seasonings (1), stir in one direction until the meat is sticky.
2. Heat the wok until very hot, add 1/2 C. oil, turn off the heat. Use the pork mixture to make 8 meat balls. Dip a spatula with oil and flatten the meat balls slightly. Turn on the heat to fry the meat (fry one side first, then turn it over to fry the other side).
3. Add shredded ginger, wine, soy sauce, and water. Cook for 5 minutes over low heat.
4. Thicken with cornstarch paste, sprinkle with green onion and sesame oil. Remove to a platter. Serve with cooked green vegetable.

鹹蛋蒸肉餅
Steamed Pork with Salted Eggs

材料：
絞肉6兩、鹹蛋2個、蔥屑1大匙

調味料：
醬油1大匙、酒1/2大匙、鹽1/4茶匙、太白粉2茶匙、水2大匙

做法：
1. 剁過之絞肉加蔥屑和調味料，仔細攪拌均勻，放入深底盤中，用手指沾水將肉的表面拍平。
2. 鹹蛋取出蛋黃，一切為二，放在肉餅上。
3. 蒸鍋的水滾後，上鍋蒸約20分鐘便可。

Ingredients：
250g. ground pork, 2 salted eggs, 1T. chopped green onion

Seasonings：
1T. soy sauce, 1/2T. wine, 1/2t. salt, 2t. cornstarch, 2T. water

Procedures：
1. Chop the ground pork for a while and mix with green onion and seasonings in a bowl. Mix thoroughly. Remove to a platter, smooth the surface with wet fingers.
2. Cut salted egg yolk in half, place on top of the meat.
3. Steam the meat for about 20 minutes. Remove and serve.

* 絞肉買回後要自己再加以剁過（吃起來肉細而有彈性）。一面剁時，可以一面加水，或者在攪拌時加水，可使肉更滑嫩。
* 亦可將1個鹹蛋白攪拌在肉料中一起蒸（不必放鹽）。
* 蒸肉餅時亦可加入切碎之醬瓜或香菇屑，以增香味，如果不放鹹蛋，亦可將切片之鹹魚（糟白魚或鹹鮭魚）放在肉上同蒸，也頗鮮美。
* Chop the pork again for a while, add some water while chopping it or while mixing it.
* You may mix a salted egg white with ground pork (Don't add salt).
* Usually, you may add chopped pickle or chopped black mushrooms to the ground pork. If you don't have salted eggs, you may steam with salted fish, which is also delicious.

燒滷豬腳
Stewed Pork Feet

材料：
豬腳1支（約1斤多）、蔥6支、薑4片、八角1顆

調味料：
深色醬油5大匙、酒1大匙、冰糖2大匙、開水4杯

做法：

1. 選擇無毛的豬腳，切成適當之大小（約4公分寬），放入開水中燙2分鐘，全部撈出，再洗淨、瀝乾。
2. 將蔥折斷後，鋪在鍋底，放下豬腳，再將八角、薑和調味料加入，先用大火煮滾，再改小火慢慢燒煮約1個半小時左右，見豬腳之皮已夠軟時，改用大火收乾一下湯汁，至有黏性便可盛出。

＊豬前腳瘦肉較多，而後腳較短，肉少而筋多。

＊ **The front feet of the pig have more meat than the back feet.**

Ingredients：
1 pork feet (about 2 lbs.), 6stalks green onion, 4 slices ginger, 1 star anise

Seasonings：
5T. dark color soy sauce, 1T. wine, 2T. rock sugar, 4C. boiling water

Procedures：

1. Cut the pork feet into pieces 4 cm" wind. Clean and boil for 2 minutes. Drain.
2. Cut the green onions in half, place in a pot. Add pork, star anise, ginger and seasonings, bring to a boil over high heat. Simmer for $1^{1}/_{2}$ hours until the skin becomes soft. If too much liquid remained, reduce it over high heat. Remove and serve.

豬肉類

22

家常獅子頭
Stewed Lion's Head

材料：
豬肉（前腿肉）1斤、豆腐（5公分四方）1塊、青江菜1斤、蔥屑1大匙

調味料
（1）水3大匙、醬油2大匙、酒1大匙、蛋1個、太白粉1大匙
（2）醬油2大匙、鹽1/2茶匙、水（或高湯）4杯

做法：
1. 將豬肉肥瘦分別切成小粒，瘦肉略加剁過後，全部放在大碗中。
2. 加入捏碎之豆腐、蔥屑及調味料（1），用力朝同一方向攪拌，同時可將絞肉抓起、往碗中摔擲，以增加肉料之彈性，見絞肉料已有黏性，便可停止。
3. 鍋中燒熱油半杯，將肉料做成4個扁形丸子，分別在油中煎黃，至外皮呈褐色即鏟起，移到砂鍋中。鍋底墊上一半炒過的青江菜。
4. 加醬油、鹽及水4杯，先用大火煮開，再改小火煮約一個半小時即可（如湯不夠，可中途加開水）。最後10分鐘時，可再加入炒過的青江菜一起燉煮。

Ingredients：
600g. pork (leg portion), 1piece bean curd (5cm×5cm),
600g. green cabbages (or Chinese cabbage), 1T. chopped green onion

Seasonings：
（1）3T. water, 2T. soy sauce, 1T. wine, 1 egg, 1T. cornstarch
（2）2T. soy sauce, 1/2t. salt, 4C. water or soup stock

Procedures：
1. Dice the pork into 0.6cm pieces, then finely chop only the lean portion of the pork. Place in a large bowl.
2. Add the mashed bean curd, green onion and the seasonings (1). Stir in one direction until the pork mixture is very sticky (about 5 minutes). Make into 4 large meat balls.
3. Heat 1/2 C. oil in wok. Fry the meat balls one by one until golden brown. Remove to a casserole dish that is already lined with stir-fried green cabbage (half portion).
4. Add soy sauce, salt, and 4C. water to the casserole dish. Bring to a boil over high heat, simmer over low heat for 1 1/2 hours (you may add water if the liquid becomes too low). Add the stir-fried green cabbage at the last 10 minutes.

∗ 本菜亦可將湯汁減少而做成紅燒獅子頭。
∗ 如嫌切肉費時，可改用絞肉，但是肉味較差。
∗ You may reduce the water, make it as a stewed dish.
∗ You may use the ground pork instead of cutting the pork.

豬肉類

糖醋豬小排
Sweet & Sour Spareribs

材料：
豬小排骨12兩、蔥3支、太白粉或蕃薯粉1/3杯

調味料：
（1）醬油2大匙、酒1/2大匙、蛋黃1個
（2）醬油2大匙、糖3大匙、鎮江醋3大匙、太白粉2茶匙、清水6大匙、麻油1茶匙

做法：
1. 將豬小排骨斬成3公分長之小塊，用調味料（1）拌勻，醃上30~40分鐘。蔥切斜絲留用。
2. 將炸油燒熱，小排骨瀝乾醬油後沾上太白粉，再投入熱油中，用中火炸約2分鐘，至肉已熟透時先撈出。
3. 將炸油重新燒熱，再放下小排骨，用大火另炸一次（約15秒鐘）、撈出。
4. 另燒熱1大匙油，將調勻的調味料（2）倒下，用大火炒煮至滾，見汁變黏稠時，熄火，將排骨和蔥絲倒入鍋中，速加拌勻，裝盤上桌。

Ingredients：
450g. pork spareribs, 3stalks green onion, 1/3C. cornstarch or sweet potato powder

Seasonings：
（1）2T. soy sauce, 1/2T. wine, 1 egg yolk
（2）2T. soy sauce, 3T. sugar, 2T. brown vinegar, 2t. corn starch, 6T. water, 1t. sesame oil

Procedures：
1. Cut the spareribs into 3cm pieces. Marinate with seasonings (1) for about 30~40 minutes. Shred the green onions.
2. Coat the spareribs with cornstarch. Deep-fry in 6C. hot oil over medium heat for 2 minutes. Remove the spareribs and reheat the oil.
3. Deep-fry the spareribs again in hot oil over high heat for only 15 seconds. Remove and drain off oil.
4. Stir-fry the seasoning sauce (2) with 1T. oil. Bring to a boil. When the sauce becomes sticky, turn off heat. Mix well with the fried spareribs and green onions. Serve.

螞蟻上樹
Minced Pork with Bean Threads

材料：
粉絲2把、絞豬肉2兩、薑屑1/2茶匙、蒜屑1茶匙、蔥屑2大匙

調味料：
辣豆瓣醬1大匙、醬油1大匙、鹽1/2茶匙、水1 1/2杯、麻油少許

做法：
1. 粉絲用冷水泡軟後瀝乾，如太長可將其切短備用。
2. 將2大匙油燒至七分熱，放下絞肉炒散，再加入薑屑、蒜屑及辣豆瓣醬續炒片刻，淋下醬油、水及鹽，待煮滾後，將粉絲放下同煮（常用鏟子翻拌）。
3. 見湯汁快要收乾時，改用大火，見粉絲透明、湯汁已乾時，撒下蔥花並淋下麻油便可裝碟。

Ingredients：
2 bundles dried bean threads, 80g. ground pork, 1/2t. chopped ginger, 1t. chopped garlic, 2T. chopped green onion

Seasonings：
1T. hot bean paste, 1T. soy sauce, 1/2t. salt, 1/4t. sesame oil

Procedures:
1. Soak the dried bean threads in water until soft. Drain and cut into sections about 6~7 cm long.
2. Stir-fry ground pork with warm oil. Add ginger, garlic, and hot bean paste, stir-fry continually. Add soy sauce, water, and salt. Bring to a boil. Add bean threads in. While the bean threads are cooking, stir it, so the threads will not stick to the wok.
3. When the liquid is reduced, sprinkle with green onions and sesame oil. Remove to a plate and serve.

* 螞蟻上樹的原始做法是將乾粉絲用油炸泡，使粉絲的形狀如同樹枝一般，因而名之。但用油炸過的粉絲吃起來很油膩，因此，現在多用水將粉絲泡軟了來做此菜。

* **Previously, many people would deep-fry the dried bean threads in hot oil, then cook them. That causes the threads to be very oily, we now only soak it.**

豬肉類

魚香蹄花
Stewed Pork Feet with Hot Sauce

材料：
豬蹄膀1個（約1斤重）、蔥3支、薑3片、八角1顆

調味料：
(1) 醬油1/2杯、酒2大匙、清水3杯
(2) 辣豆瓣醬1 1/2大匙、蒜屑1/2大匙、薑屑1茶匙、糖1/2大匙、醋1/2大匙、太白粉水2茶匙、麻油1茶匙、蔥花3大匙

做法：
1. 蹄膀連皮切成5公分四方大小，用醬油拌勻泡10分鐘，用熱油炸黃，撈出後泡入冷水，使油膩減少。
2. 將肘子放回鍋內，加入浸泡時剩下之醬油，另加蔥、薑、八角、酒及清水，用小火燒煮1小時半左右，至夠爛而汁僅餘1杯量為止。
3. 起油鍋用2大匙油炒香辣豆瓣醬及蒜、薑屑，並倒下煮蹄膀之湯汁，加入糖、醋煮滾後，淋下太白粉水勾芡，撒下蔥花、淋下麻油，即可澆到盤中之蹄花上。

Ingredients:
600g. pork (leg portion), 3 stalks green onion, 3 slices ginger, 1 star anise

Seasonings:
(1) 1/2C. soy sauce, 2T. wine, 3C. water
(2) 1 1/2T. hot bean paste, 1/2T. chopped garlic, 1t. chopped ginger, 1/2T. sugar, 1/2T. vinegar, 2t. cornstarch paste, 1t. sesame oil, 3T. chopped green onion

Procedures:
1. Cut the pork into 5cm squares. Soak with soy sauce for 10 minutes. Deep-fry in hot oil until the outside becomes golden brown. Soak in cold water for 10 minutes.
2. Put the pork in a pot, add remaining soy sauce, green onion, ginger, star anise, wine, and water. Simmer for about 1 1/2 hour. There should be about 1C. of liquid left. Remove the pork to a platter.
3. Heat 2 T. oil to stir-fry the hot bean paste, garlic, and ginger. Add the liquid, sugar, and vinegar. Bring to a boil. Thicken with cornstarch paste. Sprinkle green onion and sesame oil, pour the sauce over the pork. Serve.

爆炒豬肝
Quick Stir-fried Pork Liver

材料：

豬肝6兩、水發木耳 1/2杯、荸薺5粒、胡蘿蔔片15片、小黃瓜1條、大蒜片10片、薑片5片、蔥段15小段

調味料：

(1) 醬油1/2大匙、酒1/2大匙、太白粉1大匙、鹽、胡椒粉各1/4茶匙

(2) 醬油1大匙、酒1/2大匙、糖1/2茶匙、鹽1/4茶匙、太白粉2茶匙、麻油少許

做法：

1. 豬肝切成薄片後，用調味料（1）拌勻醃2~3分鐘，即全部倒入滾水中燙5秒鐘，馬上撈起、瀝乾。荸薺和黃瓜分別切片。
2. 起油鍋用2大匙油爆炒大蒜與薑片，並放下黃瓜片、荸薺片、胡蘿蔔片與木耳，淋下2大匙清水，用大火拌炒，加入豬肝片同炒數下。
3. 倒下調勻的調味料（2），再用大火拌炒均勻，至有黏性時即熄火。
4. 撒下蔥段，立刻盛到碟內上桌。

Ingredients：

250g. pork liver, 1/2C. black fungus, 5 water chestnuts, 15 slices carrots, 1 cucumber, 10 slices garlic, 5 slices ginger, 15 pieces green onion section

Seasonings：

(1) 1/2T. soy sauce, 1/2T. wine, 1T. cornstarch, 1/4t. salt, 1/4t. black pepper

(2) 1T. soy sauce, 1/2T. wine, 1/2t. sugar, 1/4t. salt, 2t. cornstarch, 1/4t. sesame oil

Procedures：

1. Slice the liver into thin pieces. Mix with seasonings (1) for 2~3 minutes. Boil in water for 5 seconds. Remove and drain immediately. Slice water chestnuts and cucumber.
2. Heat 3T. oil in wok, stir-fry garlic and ginger. Add vegetables, and 2T. water in, stir-fry over high heat. Add liver and stir-fry again.
3. Add the seasonings (2), stir-fry thoroughly over high heat. Turn off the heat when the liquid becomes sticky.
4. Add green onions and remove to a plate. Serve hot.

豬肉類

雞鴨類

梅醬雞

Chicken with Plum Sauce

材料：
雞腿2支、蔥3支、薑2片

調味料：
醬油1/2杯、酒2大匙、糖1大匙
五香料：花椒1大匙、八角1粒、陳皮（絲）1大匙、甘草2片
梅醬料：話梅6粒、蘇州梅10粒、冰糖4大匙

做法：

1. 將雞腿洗淨擦乾水份後，用醬油泡5分鐘。在燒得很熱的油中將雞腿表皮炸黃（要雞皮朝下放入油中），撈出。
2. 用1大匙油爆香蔥段和薑片，並加入調味料和五香料（先用白布包好）及開水4杯，將雞腿放入，用小火煮20分鐘，取出後放涼。
3. 蘇州梅與話梅加水2杯，蒸20分鐘，再加入冰糖拌合，一起用小火煮10分鐘（用叉子搗壓，盡量使梅肉脫落）。再加入煮雞之湯汁1杯半，續用小火燒煮20分鐘使其汁黏稠，用紗網過篩除去酸梅核，梅肉裝在碗中。
4. 將雞腿切成約1公分寬的長方塊、裝碟，澆上適量之梅醬供食。

Ingredients:
2 chicken legs, 3stalks green onion, 2slices ginger

Seasonings:
1/2C. soy sauce, 2T. wine, 1T. sugar

Spices：1T. brown peppercorn, 1 star anise, 1T. shredded dried orange peel, 2 piece licorice root

Plum sauce：6 dried plums, 10 preserved plums, 4T. rock sugar

Procedures:

1. Clean and pat the legs dry. Soak in soy sauce for 5 minutes. Deep-fry in hot oil until the skin side become golden brown (put the skin side down when you put the legs into the oil). Drain.
2. Heat 1T. oil to fry the green onions and ginger. Add the seasonings and 4 cups of hot water. Add the chicken legs in, cook over low heat for about 20 minutes. Remover and let it cool. Save the chicken stock for later use.
3. Steam the two kinds of plums with 2 cups of hot water for 20 minutes. Mix with rock sugar, simmer for about 20 minutes. Use a fork to mash the plums to remove the pits. Add 1 1/2cups of chicken stock, simmer for another 20 minutes until the juice becomes thicker. Save the plum sauce in a bowl.
4. Cut the chicken legs into 1cm wide pieces, place it on a serving plate and pour the plum sauce over the meat. Serve.

＊不要將剩下的雞塊和梅醬混合。餘下之梅子醬，可裝瓶存放冰箱中留用。

＊**Cut up only the amount of chicken you will be using each time. Do not store chicken and plum sauce together, as the chicken will become soggy.**

棒棒雞
Bon Bon Chicken

材料：
雞半隻、粉皮2張、小黃瓜1條、薑汁1茶匙、蒜泥2茶匙
煮雞料：蔥1支、薑2片、酒1大匙

調味料：
芝麻醬1大匙、冷開水2大匙、甜醬油2大匙、
鎮江醋1/2大匙、麻油1大匙、辣油1/2大匙、花椒粉1/4茶匙

做法：
1. 鍋中煮滾水5杯，放入雞和煮雞料，以中火煮20分鐘，撈出後使其冷卻。
2. 黃瓜切片，用少許鹽醃10分鐘，擠乾水分鋪在盤底。
3. 粉皮切成寬條，用冷開水沖洗再擦乾，拌少許麻油後放在黃瓜上，再將雞肉放在粉皮上（粉皮如隔日已變白，則需放在開水中川燙至透明，再撈出瀝乾）。
4. 剔除雞骨頭，連皮切成3~4公分長的粗條。
5. 小碗內先將芝麻醬用冷開水調開，再加入其他的調味料和薑汁、蒜泥，淋到雞肉上便可上桌。

* 甜醬油做法：醬油1 1/2杯加糖1杯、酒2大匙、蔥2支、薑1片、八角1顆、花椒10粒、陳皮1小片一起小火煮15分鐘，濾出便是。

* **If you don't have fresh bean sheets, you may use dried bean sheets. Boil the sheets in water until transparent.**

* **To make sweet soy sauce: Cook 1 1/2 C. soy sauce, 1 C. sugar, 2 T. wine, 2 stalks green onions, 1 slice ginger, 1 staranise, 1/2 T. brown peppercorn and a small piece of dried orange peel over low heat for about 15 minutes. Drain the sauce.**

Ingredients:
(1) 1/2 chicken, 2 pieces mung bean sheet, 1 small cucumber, 1t. ginger juice, 2t. mashed garlic
(2) **to cook the chicken**：1stalk green onion, 2 slices ginger, 1T. wine

Seasonings：
1T. sesame seed paste, 2T. water, 2T. sweet soy sauce,
1/2T. vinegar, 1T. sesame oil, 1/2 T. red chili oil,
1/4t. brown peppercorn powder

Procedures:
1. Cook the chicken with 5 cups of boiling water and ingredients (2) over medium heat for about 20 minutes. Remove and let cool.
2. Slice the cucumber. Mix with 1/4t.salt and let stand for 10 minutes. Squeeze excess water out and place on the serving plate.
3. Cut mung bean sheets into 2cm wide, rinse and mix with 1/2 t. sesame oil. Place it over the cucumber.
4. Remove chicken bones. Cut the meat into pieces 3.5cm long×0.5cm wide—about the width of a chopstick. Place the meat on top of the mung bean sheets.
5. Mix the sesame seed paste with water. Add the other sauces, then mix with ginger and garlic. Pour the sauce over the chicken, mix at the table just before eating.

三杯雞
Three Cups Chicken

材料：

雞1/2隻（約1 1/2斤重）、大蒜7~8粒、薑10片、紅辣椒2支、九層塔3支

調味料：

麻油1/2杯、米酒1杯、醬油1/4杯、糖1茶匙

做法：

1. 將雞洗淨內部後，斬成3公分長方形塊狀。
2. 鍋先燒熱，再將麻油燒至七、八分熱，放下大蒜及薑片（最好用老薑）爆香，再將雞塊入鍋以大火煸炒至雞塊變白沒有血水時，才加入米酒、醬油和糖，大火煮開。
3. 蓋上鍋蓋，以小火燜至雞塊熟透且湯汁僅剩不到半杯為止即可。

＊ 要選擇較小的雞，最好是半土雞或放山雞。早期做法是3種調味料各1杯，但會太鹹，現在都加以調整了。

＊ 本菜可按個人喜愛，加入中藥補品一同燒煮，做為進補之用。

Ingredients:

1/2 chicken (2 lbs.), 7~8 cloves garlic, 10 slices ginger, 2 red chili , 3 stalks basil

Seasonings:

1/2C. sesame oil, 1C. wine, 1/4C. soy sauce, 1t. sugar

Procedures:

1. Clean the chicken and cut into pieces 3 cm wide. Heat a casserole dish, add sesame oil and heat again. Stir-fried garlic and ginger until brown. Add chicken and stir-fry over high heat until the chicken turns white. Add wine , soy sauce, and suger. Bring to a boil.
2. Cover and cook for about 20 minutes until done. Serve in the casserole dish.

＊ The traditional way is to add one cup of each seasoning, now we usually want to reduce the salttaste.

＊ Chinese medicine herbs may added if you prefer.

雞鴨類

五香滷雞

Braised Chicken with Spicy Brown Sauce

材料：
雞1隻、五香包1包（約半兩）

調味料：
醬油1杯、酒半杯、冰糖2大匙、鹽2茶匙

做法：
1. 鍋中煮開10杯水，放下調味料及五香包，以小火煮30分鐘即為滷汁（新滷）。
2. 雞洗淨後放入滷汁中，先用大火煮滾（煮時用一支大湯勺將湯汁往雞身上淋澆），滾後改為小火，蓋上鍋蓋再煮約10分鐘。
   將雞翻一面，再蓋上鍋蓋煮8分鐘，便可將火關掉，將雞燜在滷湯中，約30分鐘
3. 後取出雞，待稍冷後，在表面上塗少許麻油。食用時按所需的量，斬切成長塊，拼盤供食。

Ingredients:
1 chicken, 1pack of five spice pack

Seasonings：
1 C. soy sauce, 1/2 C. wine, 2T. rock sugar, 2 t. salt,

Procedures:
1. Put the seasonings and the five spice pack into a large pot of boiling water (about 10 cups). Cook over low heat for 1/2 hour until the aroma of the spices is strong. This is the spicy brown sauce.
2. Clean the chicken. Add it to the spicy brown sauce and bring to a boil (spoon the sauce over the chicken for a few minutes). Cover the pot and simmer for 10 minutes over low heat.
3. Turn the chicken over and simmer for another 8 minutes. Turn off the heat. Let the chicken soak in the sauce for 30 minutes. Remove from pot. When the chicken cools a little, brush the surface with a little of sesame oil. Cut the amount you want to serve into pieces 1" wide and arrange on a plate.

* 滷汁待涼後就可放進冰箱中冷凍存放，要再滷食物時，只要將要滷的東西洗淨便可放入滷鍋中滷，不同的食材滷好後都要浸泡使之入味。
* 滷湯如變少不夠時，可酌量加水及醬油、酒、糖，數次之後，可再換一個新的五香包。五香包一般包括八角、桂皮、陳皮、花椒、丁香、小茴、茴香、甘草、沙薑、草果（豆蔻）等。滷湯不用時可冷凍存放。
* **You can frozen the sauce in the refrigerator, whenever you want to reuse the sauce, place the ingredients and sauce into a pan and reheat.**
* **When the amount of sauce gets too low, just add water and seasonings. After several uses, change to a new five spice pack. This can be pur chased in a Chinese drugstore or super market, and actually contains about 10 different Chinese spices. It include star anise, cinnamon, dried orange peel, brown pepper corn, cloves, cumin, fennel, licorice root, dried ginger and nutmeg. Wrap the spices in a piece of cheesecloth. The sauce will keep for years if you frozen it. If you cannot obtain these spices, ginger and green onion may be substituted.**

雞鴨類

34

琥珀雞凍
Jellied Chicken

材料：
雞腿3支、豬肉皮4兩（或膠粉15公克）、蔥2支、薑2片、八角1顆

調味料：
醬油4大匙、酒1大匙、糖1/2大匙、鹽1/3茶匙

做法：
1. 將雞腿洗淨，連骨剁成小塊；豬肉皮刮淨後切成約4公分四方大小，一起放入開水中燙約半分鐘，撈出洗淨、瀝乾。
2. 將燙過的雞塊和肉皮一起放在鍋中，加其他材料及調味料與開水6杯，先用大火燒滾，立即改用小火煮約30分鐘。將雞塊先揀出，放在一個大碗內。
3. 豬皮撈出剁成小粒，再放回鍋中，用小火續煮10分鐘使湯汁黏稠、約剩2杯。
4. 用細紗網將湯汁過濾至大碗中，待涼透後，再放入冰箱內冷藏，約4～5小時，湯汁即可凝固。
5. 食用時以湯匙挖成小塊，裝入碟內（凝固後表面之油脂要刮除不要）。

Ingredients：
3 chicken legs, 150g. pork skin (or 2 packs unflavored gelatin), 2 stalks green onions, 2 slices ginger, 1 star anise

Seasonings：
5 T. soy sauce, 1T. wine, 1/2 T. sugar, 1/2 t. salt

Procedures:
1. Clean and cut the chicken legs into small pieces. Cut the pork skin into 4cm squares. Put it both into 6 cups of boiling water. Boil for 2 minutes. Drain and place them in a pot.
2. Add other ingredients, the seasonings, and 6C. water. Bring to a boil. Simmer for 30 minutes. Remove the chicken and put it into a large bowl.
3. Chop the pork skin and put it back into the pot. Simmer for another 10 minutes, until the sauce becomes thicker (there should be about 2C. sauce left).
4. Strain the sauce into the bowl with the chicken. When it cools, place in the refrigerator for about 4~5 hours, until it sets.
5. Use spoon to separate the chicken, and transfer onto a serving plate (skin off grease from surface after it becomes firm).

* 為使雞凍顏色透明，煮時需用小火慢煮，湯汁不能混濁。
* 雞凍可放置數日，故一次可多做些，分次食用，亦可用雞翅膀或豬腳來做。
* 使用膠粉時則先用1杯冷水溶化再倒入做法（3）的熱湯汁中攪勻。

* **Use very low heat in order to keep the sauce clear.**
* **You may use chicken wings or pork instead of chicken legs.**
* **If you use unflavored gelatin, mix it with 1 C. cold water and then add it into hot chicken sauce in #3. Bring to a boil.**

左公雞
Stir-fried Chicken, Hunan Style

材料：
雞胸1個或雞腿2支、青椒1/2個、紅辣椒2支、大蒜6粒

調味料：
（1）醬油2茶匙、太白粉1/2大匙、水1大匙
（2）醬油1大匙、酒1大匙、太白粉1/2茶匙、水2大匙
（3）醋1茶匙、麻油1/4茶匙

做法：
1. 雞去骨後切成長條小塊，用調味料（1）醃20分鐘。
2. 青椒及紅辣椒去籽，切成塊；大蒜切片。
3. 先將鍋燒熱後，放入1杯油，待油達至九分熱時，便可將雞肉倒入鍋中，大火過油，炸至雞肉轉為白色，撈出。將油倒出，僅餘2大匙在鍋中。
4. 用大火先爆炒大蒜片及青紅辣椒，至青椒微軟時，倒下雞丁同炒數下，淋下調味料（2），大火拌炒均勻，起鍋前淋下醋及麻油。

＊ 這道菜是正宗的湖南名菜，左公即左宗棠先生，本菜特點是雞肉香、嫩。

＊ **This is a very famous Hunan dish.**
＊ **The chicken is very tender and delicious.**

Ingredients:
1 piece chicken breast or 2 chicken legs, 1/2 green pepper, 2 red pepper, 6 cloves garlic

Seasonings:
（1）2t. soy sauce, 1/2T. cornstarch, 1T. water
（2）1T. soy sauce, 1T. wine, 1/2 t. cornstarch, 2T. water
（3）1t. vinegar, 1/4t. sesame oil

Procedures:
1. Remove all bones from chicken, cut into small pieces. Marinate with seasonings (1) for 20 minutes.
2. Remove the seeds from both the green pepper and red chili. Cut into cubes. Slice the garlic cloves.
3. Heat the wok until very hot, add 1 C. oil, heat to 180°C, fry the chicken until the meat turns white. Drain.
4. In 2T. oil, quickly stir-fry garlic and green pepper. Add chicken and red chili, stir-fry for another 10 seconds. Pour in the seasoning (2) and mix thoroughly. Sprinkle vinegar and sesame oil on top and remove from heat immediately.

紅燒雞
Stewed Chicken with Brown Sauce

材料：
雞1/2隻、筍2支、蔥3支、薑2片

調味料：
醬油4大匙、酒1大匙、糖1大匙、水3杯

做法：
1. 將雞剁成約5公分長、2.5公分寬之長方塊，用滾水川燙一下；筍切成比雞塊小一點的滾刀塊狀。
2. 用2大匙油將蔥段、薑片炒香，放入雞塊和筍塊再同炒一下，加入所有調味料。
3. 先用大火煮滾，再改用小火慢慢燜燒，約燒1小時，最後用大火收乾湯汁。（此時需常常提起鍋子輕輕搖動，或用鏟子輕輕翻動，以免雞肉黏鍋底）。

Ingredients:
1/2 chicken, 2 bamboo shoots, 3 stalks green onion, 2 slices ginger

Seasonings:
4T. soy sauce, 1T. wine, 1T. sugar, 3C. water

Procedure:
1. Cut into pieces 5cm long and 2.5cm wide. Blanch and drain. Cut the bamboo shoots into cubes.
2. Heat 2T. oil to stir-fry green onion and ginger, add chicken and bamboo shoot in, stir-fry a little, add the seasonings. Bring to a boil, then simmer for about 1 hour. When
3. chicken is almost done, use high heat to reduce the liquid (shake the wok gently so the chicken will not stick to the bottom).

* 筍子可按不同季節用冬筍或綠竹筍等。在紅燒雞時，亦可放香菇、馬鈴薯、百頁結、芋頭、洋菇、油豆腐、栗子等，均可增加雞的美味。

* 傳統紅燒雞時會將雞先用蔥、薑和醬油醃泡10分鐘，並用熱油將它炸黃後紅燒，亦可嘗試。

* **You may add other vegetables when stewing the chicken, such as: black mushrooms, potatoes, taro, mushrooms, fried tofu, or chestnuts.**

* **The traditional way to stew chicken is marinate the chicken with green onion, ginger and soy sauce for 10 minutes, deep-fry it in heated oil then stew. You may try that way.**

雞鴨類

銀芽雞絲
Stir-fried Chicken Shreds

材料：
雞胸肉1片（約4兩）、綠豆芽6兩、紅辣椒1支、嫩薑絲1大匙

調味料：
（1）鹽1/4茶匙、水1大匙、太白粉1/2大匙、蛋白1個
（2）鹽1/4茶匙、雞粉少許、醬油1茶匙、酒1/2大匙

做法：
1. 將雞胸剔除雞皮與白筋，放冷凍室中冰硬一些，再將雞肉片切成大薄片，順絲切成約5公分長細絲。將調味料（1）調好在碗中，放下雞絲輕輕抓拌均勻，醃約20分鐘。
2. 綠豆芽摘去尾根，洗淨瀝乾；紅辣椒去籽、切細絲。
3. 將1杯油熱至六分熱時，放下雞肉，馬上用筷子撥散，在油中泡至雞肉變白，即可撈出、瀝淨油。
4. 另用2大匙油以大火來炒薑絲、紅辣椒絲及綠豆芽，撒下鹽及雞粉，隨即放入雞絲，並烹上酒和醬油增香，拌勻便可裝盤。

Ingredients：
1 piece chicken breast, 240g. bean sprouts, 2 red chili, 2T. ginger shreds

Seasonings：
(1) 1/2t. salt, 1T. water, 1/2T. cornstarch, 2T. egg white
(2) 1/2t. salt, a pinch of chicken powder, 1t. soy sauce, 1/2T. wine

Procedures：
1. Remove all the bones and skin from chicken breast Put it into the freezer for about 20 minutes.. Shred it finely into 5cm long. Gently mix with marinade sauce, and let stand for 20 minutes.
2. Trim the bean sprouts；shred the red chili.
3. Heat 1C. oil to 120°C, add chicken and stir it separately with a pair of chopsticks until chicken turns white. Drain.
4. Heat 2T. oil to stir-fry ginger, red chili and bean sprouts. Season with salt and chicken powder. Add chicken in and sprinkle with wine and soy sauce to enhance the flavor. Mix well and transfer to a serving plate.

鹽酥雞塊
Deep-fried Crispy Chicken

材料：
雞半隻（或雞腿2支）、蔥2支、薑2片、蕃薯粉2/3杯

調味料：
（1）酒1大匙、鹽1/4茶匙、蛋黃1個
（2）五香粉1/2茶匙、白胡椒粉1/2茶匙、鹽1茶匙、
　　大蒜 粉1茶匙

做法：
1. 將雞的大骨去掉後，斬成3公分左右的雞塊，放在大碗中，加入拍碎的蔥、薑及調味料（1）一起拌勻，醃約20分鐘。
2. 雞肉中加入蕃薯粉拌勻，儘量使每塊雞肉均裹上蕃薯粉，再把雞肉投入燒熱的油中炸熟，待雞炸至八分熟時，先撈出一次，將油再燒熱，重落雞下鍋，以大火再炸半分鐘，以至外表酥脆。
3. 乾淨的鍋燒熱，放入雞塊，均勻撒下調味料（2），小火拌炒均勻後裝盤。

* 可以炸一些九層塔拌在雞塊中。

Ingredients：
1/2 chicken(or 2 chicken legs), 2 stalks green onion,
2 slices ginger, 2/3C. sweet potato powder

Seasonings：
（1）1T. wine, 1/4t. salt, 1 egg yolk
（2）1/2t. five spice powder, 1/2t. white pepper, 1t. salt,
　　1t. garlic powder

Procedures：
1. Remove the large bones from the chicken, then cut it into 3cm cubes. Mix evenly with the smashed green onions and ginger, add seasonings (1), marinate for 20 minutes.
2. Mix sweet potato powder with the chicken. Coat it well. Deep-fry it in heated oil until almost done. Remove chicken, reheat the oil and deep-fry again over high heat until the outside becomes very crispy, about 1/2 minute.
3. Heat a clean dry wok. Put the chicken back to the wok. Sprinkle the seasonings (2), mix thoroughly over low heat. Serve.

* **You may deep-fry some basil leaves, mix it with fried chicken to enhance the flavor.**

醬爆雞丁
Chicken with Sweet Soy Bean Paste

材料：
雞腿2支、黃瓜1條、紅辣椒2支、蔥1支、大蒜3粒

調味料：
（1）醬油1大匙、水2大匙、太白粉1大匙
（2）甜麵醬1大匙、糖2茶匙、麻油1/2茶匙、醬油1/2大匙、水3大匙

做法：
1. 雞腿去骨，用刀在雞肉上輕輕剁過（使肉鬆嫩且醃時較易入味），再切成1公分四方大小，用調味料（1）拌勻，醃20分鐘左右。
2. 黃瓜切成1公分四方小丁；紅辣椒去籽後亦切成小丁；蔥切小斜段；大蒜切片；調味料（2）先調勻。
3. 2杯油燒至八分熱，倒下雞丁大火泡熟，再將黃瓜及紅辣椒一起下鍋，約5秒鐘即可撈出，瀝乾油汁。
4. 另熱2大匙油，爆香蔥段及大蒜片，再加入調味料（2）炒至香味透出，倒下雞丁等大火炒勻便可盛出。

＊此菜取甜麵醬之香，因此要在油中將醬料炒透，炒時火力不能太大，以免醬焦有苦味。

＊**The taste of soy bean paste is very important for this dish, stir-fry it over medium heat to avoid from getting burned.**

Ingredients：
2 chicken legs, 1 small cucumber, 2 red chilies, 1stalk green onion, 3 cloves garlic

Seasonings：
（1）1T. soy sauce, 2T. water, 1T. cornstarch
（2）1T. sweet soy bean paste, 2t. sugar, 1/2t. sesame oil, 1/2T. soy sauce, 3T. water

Procedures：
1. Remove bones from the chicken. Use a cleaver to gently pound the meat, then cut it into 1cm cubes. Marinate with seasonings (1) for 20 minutes.
2. Cut cucumber into 1cm cubes；remove seeds from red chilies and dice it；cut green onion into sections；slice the garlic cloves；mix seasonings (2) in a bowl.
3. Heat 2C. of oil to 160ºC, stir-fry chicken in hot oil for about 20 seconds, add cucumber and red chili in, fry for 5 seconds. Drain all the ingredients.
4. Heat another 2T. of oil to stir-fry green onion and garlic. Add soy bean mixture and stir-fry over medium heat until you can smell the bean paste. Add chicken and stir-fry over high heat, mixing thoroughly. Transfer onto a serving plate.

香酥雞腿
Crispy Chicken Legs

材料：
棒棒雞腿6支、蔥2支、薑3片、花椒粒2大匙、麵粉1/2杯

調味料：
鹽2茶匙、酒1大匙、醬油2大匙

做法：

1. 在一只乾鍋中以小火慢慢炒香花椒粒，再加入鹽同炒至鹽微黃即盛入大碗中，加入拍碎之蔥、薑及酒拌勻。
2. 用蔥薑料醃雞腿，放置約2~3小時。放入電鍋中蒸1小時半至雞腿夠爛。
3. 在蒸爛的雞腿上抹一層醬油，並拍上一層麵粉，隨即投入已燒熱之炸油中，以大火炸成金黃色（亦可撈出雞腿，將油燒熱，再入鍋大火炸酥）。撈出瀝乾油漬、裝盤。

Ingredients：
6 chicken legs, 2 stalks green onion, 3 slices ginger, 2T. brown peppercorn, 1/2C. flour

Seasonings：
2t. salt, 1T. wine, 2T. soy sauce

Procedures：

1. Stir-fry the brown peppercorns over low heat in a clean wok for a few seconds until fragrant. Add salt and continue to stir-fry until the salt becomes light brown. Remove to a large bowl. Add wine, crushed green onions and ginger. Mix together thoroughly.
2. Marinate chicken legs with brown peppercorn mixture for 2~3 hours. Steam it in rice cooker for about 1 1/2 hours until very tender.
3. Wipe the chicken legs dry. Brush soy sauce over the legs and coat it with flour. Deep-fry in hot oil until brown and crispy (it is much better to deep-fry it twice). Drain and arrange on a plate.

雞鴨類

蔥油淋雞腿
Steamed Chicken with Green Onion Sauce

材料：
雞腿2支、蔥絲1/2杯、薑絲1/2杯

調味料：
鹽1茶匙、酒1大匙、蔥1支、薑2片

做法：
1. 雞腿洗淨，用叉子在雞腿上刺數下，以使醃泡時易入味。將鹽與酒混合後，加拍碎的蔥、薑拌合，用來在雞腿上摩擦搓捏，醃約20分鐘。
2. 蒸鍋中之水燒開後，放下雞腿，大火蒸約12分鐘，熄火後再燜5分鐘。將雞腿取出，在乾淨菜板上，將每隻雞腿剁成5塊，排列盤中。
3. 把切好的蔥絲及薑絲（切好在冷開水中浸泡著）撒在雞腿上。2大匙油燒得極熱後，淋在蔥薑上，並再淋下3大匙蒸雞之汁，即可上桌。

Ingredients：
2 chicken legs, 1/2C. ginger shreds, 1/2C. green onion shreds

Seasonings：
1t. salt, 1T. wine, 1stalk green onion, 2 slices ginger

Procedures：
1. Crush the green onion and ginger slices, mix with salt and wine. Clean the chicken legs and rub with the green onion mixture. Marinate for 20 minutes.
2. Steam the chicken legs for 12 minutes over high heat. Turn off the heat and let chicken remain in steamer for another 5 minutes. Cut into 5 pieces per leg. Arrange on platter.
3. Sprinkle the shredded green onion and ginger on top. Heat 2T. oil, pour the heated oil over the green onion and ginger, also pour 3 T. of chicken broth (remaining from steamed chicken) over, then serve.

﹡雞塊淋過油後，也可將油泌回炒鍋內，與雞汁混合煮滾、勾芡，再澆到雞腿上。

﹡ **You may pour the oil back to wok after pouring over chicken, reheat with. chicken broth, thicken with cornstarch paste, then pour over chicken again.**

豉汁蒸雞球
Chicken with Fermented Black Beans

材料：

雞腿2支、太白粉2大匙、豆豉1/2大匙、大蒜屑2大匙、紅辣椒粒1大匙、蔥屑1大匙

調味料：

酒1大匙、鹽1/4茶匙、糖1/2茶匙、淡色醬油1大匙

做法：

1. 雞腿洗淨、除去腿骨，用刀尖在雞肉上輕輕斬切（尤其是有白筋的部分，要使白筋斬斷、才不會縮），再切成3公分大小的塊狀，用太白粉拌勻。
2. 燒熱1大匙油，放入泡軟的豆豉及大蒜屑，用小火炒香，淋下酒和調味料拌勻，關火後再把雞肉拌入，馬上盛到盤中。將雞塊攤平，並撒下紅辣椒粒。
3. 用大火蒸約15分鐘即可取出，將雞肉換到一個乾淨的盤中，撒下蔥粒，澆上燒熱的1大匙油便可上桌。

*用同樣的方法，可以做豉汁魚片、豉汁肉片、豉汁排骨等不同菜式。唯魚片較易熟，僅需蒸10分鐘就可以了。

*You may substitute fish fillets or spareribs for the chicken. If you use fish, you only steam it for 10 minutes.

Ingredients：

2 chicken legs, 2T. cornstarch, 1/2T. fermented black beans, 2T. chopped garlic, 1T. chopped red chiili, 1T. chopped green onion

Seasonings：

1T. wine, 1/4t. salt, 1/2t. sugar, 1T. soy sauce

Procedures：

1. Remove the bones from legs. Chop the meat with the blade of the cleaver a few times (cut through the chicken tendons), cut it into 3cm cubes. Mix with cornstarch.
2. Heat 1T. oil to stir-fry fermented black beans (these should already be soaked) and chopped garlic over low heat. Add seasonings, turn off heat. Add chicken in, mix well and place on platter, spreading it evenly. Sprinkle chopped red chili on top.
3. Steam chicken over high heat for 15 minutes. Transfer the chicken onto a serving platter, sprinkling it with chopped green onion and 1T. heated oil. Serve.

雞鴨類

金針雲耳雞
Stewed Chicken, Country Style

材料：
雞半隻、乾木耳1大匙、金針30支、筍1支、蔥1支、薑3片

調味料：
醬油5大匙、酒1大匙、糖1/2茶匙、鹽1/3茶匙、太白粉水少許

做法：
1. 雞先用醬油泡約20分鐘。用熱油炸至表面呈金黃色，撈出。
2. 木耳和金針分別用水泡軟，木耳要摘蒂、洗淨，金針則每2支結成一條；筍切片。
3. 用2大匙油先將蔥、薑煎香，加入木耳、金針及筍炒過，淋下剩下之醬油、酒，並加糖、鹽及熱水3杯，把雞放下，蓋鍋燒煮約20分鐘（先用大火煮滾後改小火）至雞熟為止，將雞撈出。
4. 用漏勺將金針等撈出，先放在盤底，再將雞除去大骨後切成1.5公分寬的塊狀，放在金針上，再把湯汁勾芡，澆在雞肉上便可。

Ingredients：
1 small chicken, 1T. dried black fungus, 30 pieces dried lily flower, 1 bamboo shoot, 1stalk green onion, 3 slices ginger

Seasonings：
5T. soy sauce, 1T. wine, 1/2t. sugar, 1/3t. salt, a little of cornstarch paste

Procedures：
1. Soak the chicken in soy sauce for 20 minutes, deep-fry in hot oil until golden brown.
2. Soak black wood ear and dried lily flower in warm water until soft. Tie two lily flowers together in a knot. Slice the bamboo shoot.
3. Fry the green onion and ginger with 2 T. oil. Add the black wood ear, lily flowers, and bamboo shoots. Stir-fry for 30 seconds, then add remaining soy sauce, wine, sugar, salt, and 3C. hot water. Add chicken in and stew for 20 minutes (bring to a boil over high heat, then turn to low heat) until chicken is done. Remove chicken.
4. Strain the other ingredients, placing them on a serving platter. Remove large bones from chicken. Cut the chicken into pieces 1.5cm wide. Place the chicken on top of the ingredients. Add the cornstarch paste to make the liquid thicker. Pour the sauce over the chicken.

＊金針與木耳均有食補功效，常食可治消腫、頭暈、耳鳴（金針）並利潤腸、止血（木耳）。

＊Fungus and lily flowers are very healthy. If you eat lily flowers regularly, they help to alleviate dizziness and ringing in your ears. Fungus helps food to digest more rapidly.

八寶封雞腿
Steamed Chicken Pudding

材料：
雞腿2支、蔥屑1大匙、香菇丁2大匙、香腸丁2大匙、蝦米丁1大匙、糯米飯3碗

調味料：
(1) 醬油2大匙
(2) 醬油2大匙、酒1大匙、糖1茶匙、胡椒粉1/4茶匙、清湯1/2杯

做法：
1. 雞腿抹上2大匙醬油後用熱油炸黃（約半分鐘）。待稍涼後，剔除大骨，將雞肉向外翻開攤平，每支腿剁成4塊，雞皮向下，平鋪在麵碗（或小盆）中。
2. 燒熱2大匙油，炒香蔥屑及香菇、香腸、蝦米等，並將2/3量的調味料（2）淋入鍋中，拌勻即熄火。
3. 再將糯米飯放入拌勻，一起填塞到碗內（雞肉上面），壓緊，再由碗邊淋下剩餘的調味料（2），即可上鍋大火蒸30分鐘。
4. 將蒸好之雞腿扣出在盤中，撒下香菜屑即可上桌。

  ＊用2杯糯米加1 1/2杯水可煮出3杯糯米飯。

  ＊**When using an electric rice cooker, add 1 1/2 C. water to 2 C. glutinous rice. You will get 3 C. of cooked glutinous rice.**

Ingredients：
2 chicken legs, 1T. chopped green onion,
2T. black mushrooms (soaked and diced), 2T. ham, diced,
1T. dried shrimp (soaked and diced),
3C. cooked glutinous rice

Seasonings：
(1) 2T. soy sauce
(2) 2T. soy sauce, 1T. wine, 1t. sugar, 1/4t. pepper, 1/2C. soup stock

Procedures：
1. Brush soy sauce on chicken legs, deep-fry in hot oil over high heat for 1/2 minutes, drain. After it cools, remove the bones. Cut each leg into 4 pieces. Arrange one leg in a bowl (skin side down), make 2 bowls.
2. Stir-fry green onion, black mushrooms, ham, and dried shrimp with 2T. oil until fragrant. Pout in 2/3 of the seasonings (2), turn off the heat.
3. Add cooked glutinous rice in. Mix thoroughly. Put the glutinous rice into the bowl on top of chicken. Add the remaining seasonings (2). Steam for 30 minutes over high heat.
4. Place a serving plate over the bowl and carefully turn both the plate and bowl over so that the chicken pudding is on the serving plate. Remove bowl. Serve.

冬菜鴨
Steamed Duck with Salted Cabbage

材料：
鴨1/2隻、冬菜2大匙、筍2支、薑3片、蔥2支、薑3片

調味料：
醬油1大匙、鹽酌量、太白粉水2茶匙

做法：

1. 鴨整塊用滾水燙1分鐘，再另換清水4杯，加蔥、薑煮半小時。取出待稍涼後斬成4公分長、1 1/2公分寬。
2. 在一個大湯碗內舖好冬菜，上面排列鴨塊（皮向下）及切成條的筍子，再注入2杯煮鴨之湯，並放薑3片，上鍋蒸1小時半左右。
3. 湯汁倒在炒鍋中，將鴨扣在水盤內，如有需要，再加醬油及鹽調味，勾芡後淋回鴨肉上便可。

＊本菜也可以多加湯而成為一道湯菜。
＊You may add more soup to make this dish as a soup.

Ingredients：
1/2 duck, 2T. salted cabbage, 2 bamboo shoots, 3 slices ginger, 2 stalks green onion

Seasonings：
1T. soy sauce, 3 slices ginger, salt, 2t. cornstarch paste

Procedures：

1. Blanch the duck for 1 minute, rinse. Cook with 4C. hot water for 1/2 hour (add green onions and ginger to the water). Remove. After it cools, cut the duck into pieces 4cm long × 1 1/2cm wide.
2. Place the salted cabbage in a large bowl. Arrange the duck pieces on top with skin side down. Cut the bamboo shoots into 1/4" sticks, place it on top of the duck, add 3 slices ginger and 2 C. of duck soup in. Steam for 1 1/2 hours.
3. Pour off and reserve the liquid. Turn the bowl carefully over onto a large platter. Remove the bowl. Put the liquid in a saucepan. Add soy sauce and salt (if necessary). Thicken with cornstarch paste. Pour the sauce over the duck and serve.

雞鴨類

什錦扒肥鴨
Stewed Duck with Assorted Vegetables

材料：
光鴨1/2隻、鴨肫肝各1個、香菇3朵、筍1支、胡蘿蔔片10片、豌豆莢15片、蔥1支、八角1顆

調味料：
深色醬油4大匙、酒1大匙、糖1茶匙、開水6杯、太白粉水1大匙、麻油少許

做法：
1. 鴨洗淨後，用醬油及酒醃上20分鐘，使鴨皮呈醬油色，然後放在熱油中，以大火將鴨皮炸黃（約1分鐘左右），撈出、瀝乾，將油倒出。
2. 利用鍋內的餘油約1大匙，將泡鴨剩下之醬油、酒倒入，再加入蔥、八角及糖，並注入開水6杯，放下鴨子（水要蓋過鴨子），先用大火煮開，再改小火燒煮，約2小時至湯汁剩下2杯左右。
3. 將鴨肫除去白筋後，切薄片；鴨肝煮熟後亦切薄片；筍與胡蘿蔔煮熟與泡軟之香菇均分別切成片狀；豌豆莢剪角備用。
4. 鴨煮爛後撈出，並將大骨拆除，把鴨平放在盤內。鍋中湯內之蔥、八角等物撈棄，將第三項之各料放入煮滾，用太白粉水勾芡，淋下少許麻油便可澆在鴨肉上。

Ingredients：
1/2 duck, 1 duck gizzard, 1 duck liver, 3 black mushrooms, 1 bamboo shoot, 10 slices carrot, 15 snow pea pots, 2 stalks green onion, 1 star anise

Seasonings：
4T. dark color soy sauce, 1T. wine, 1t. sugar, 6C. hot water, 1T. cornstarch paste, a few drops of sesame oil

Procedures：
1. Clean duck. Marinate with soy sauce and wine for 20 minutes, deep-fry in hot oil until the skin becomes brown (about 1 minutes). Remove the duck and drain off the oil.
2. Only keep 1T. oil in the wok, add the remaining soy sauce and wine, put green onions, star anise, sugar, and hot water in wok, place the duck in. Bring to a boil over high heat, then simmer for about 2 hours until only 2C. of broth is left.
3. Remove the ligaments of the gizzard, and slice. Cook the liver, carrots, and bamboo shoot. Soak the black mushrooms to soft, slice them separately. Trim the snow pea pots.
4. Lay the duck on a serving platter with the large breast bone removed. Remove the crumbs and spices from the stewed sauce. Add sliced ingredients in, cook until done. Thicken with cornstarch paste. Sprinkle with sesame oil and pour over duck, serve.

* 什錦材料可按個人喜好選擇，只要顏色稍有變化、任何材料皆可。

* **Any kind of vegetable may be stewed with the duck, keeping in mind that the dish should be colorful.**

芹菜拌鴨條
Roasted Duck Salad

材料：

燒鴨1/4隻、芹菜4兩

調味料：

芥末粉1/2大匙、清水2大匙、芝麻醬1/2大匙、淡色醬油1大匙、清湯1大匙、糖1/2茶匙、鹽1/2茶匙、麻油1茶匙

做法：

1. 將燒鴨（鴨胸或鴨腿皆可）骨剔除，鴨肉切成5公分長之粗條（如竹筷頭粗細）。
2. 芹菜摘除葉子及根後，放入開水（約6杯，水中加鹽1茶匙）中燙10秒鐘左右（如用西芹，可先切成條再公分長，放在盤中鴨條旁。
3. 小碗中盛裝芥末粉，加清水調成糊狀，放在溫熱處約2分鐘即可取用（可用膏狀綠色山葵代替）。
4. 另用小碗將各項調味料調勻，再與芥末汁混合均勻上桌，臨食時澆在鴨肉上即可。

Ingredients:

1/4 roasted duck (breast or leg), 150g. celery

Seasonings：

1/2T. mustard powder, 2T. water, 1/2T. sesame seed paste, 1T. soy sauce, 1T. soup stock, 1/2t. sugar, 1/4t. salt1, 1/4t. sesame oil

Procedures：

1. Remove the bones from the duck. Cut into pieces 5cmlong and 1/4" wide.
2. Trim the celery and boil in water with 1t. salt for 10 seconds (if the wide stalk celery is used, be sure to cut into pieces 0.6cm wide). Remove and rinse with cold water. Squeeze excess moisture out and cut into pieces 4cm long. Arrange the duck pieces and celery on a plate.
3. Mix the mustard powder and water in a small bowl. Put in a warm place for 2 minutes. (You may use green wasabi instead yellow mustard powder.)
4. Mix the seasoning sauce in another small bowl, and mix this mixture with the mustard thoroughly. Pour over duck before eating.

胡蔥鴨
Stewed Duck with Scallion

材料：
鴨1/2隻、大蔥2支、酸菜半棵

調味料：
醬油1/2杯、酒1大匙、開水8杯、鹽少許

做法：

1. 將鴨洗淨，擦乾水分，用醬油3大匙塗抹鴨皮，以使鴨皮能沾上醬油顏色。
2. 將油燒熱，放下鴨子以大火油炸，待鴨表皮顏色呈很均勻的褐色時撈出。
3. 用1大匙油將切成5公分長段的大蔥煎香，淋下酒，再將醬油亦倒進，注入開水、放下鴨子，煮滾後，以中小火燜燒1小時左右。
4. 酸菜洗淨，將大片的葉子鋪在砂鍋裏，酸菜心切斜片也放入砂鍋內，再將鴨子連湯移進砂鍋中，續用小火煮至鴨肉夠爛（約1小時左右），加酌量的鹽調味後，便可連鍋上桌供食。

Ingredients：
1/2 duck, 2 stalks scallion, 1/2 pickled mustard

Seasonings：
1/2C. soy sauce, 1T. wine, 8C. boiling water, salt

Procedures：

1. Clean the duck and pat it dry. Brush the skin with 3T. soy sauce until the skin becomes brown.
2. Heat the oil to very hot. Deep-fry the duck over high heat. When the skin becomes evenly brown, remove.
3. Stir-fry the scallions (cut into pieces 5cm long) with 1T. oil. Add wine, the remaining soy sauce and water. Place the duck in, bring to a boil. Cook over low heat for 1 hour.
4. Rinse the pickled mustard and cut into large pieces. Place in a casserole dish. Add the duck and soup in, simmer until the duck is tender enough (about 1 hour). Season with some salt. Serve in the casserole dish.

＊沒有大蔥的季節，可以用較粗的蔥代替，大蔥較甜。以胡蔥鴨之湯汁來煨麵條，風味頗佳。

＊ **You may use green onion instead of scallions. It's very delicious to cook noodles with the duck soup.**

燴鴨絲羹
Duck Potage

材料：
燒鴨或鹽水鴨4兩、竹笙4支、香菇2朵、筍1支、熟火腿絲1大匙、蔥1支、嫩薑2片、高湯2½杯、香菜2支

調味料：
醬油2大匙、酒1大匙、鹽1茶匙、麻油少許、濕太白粉1½大匙

做法：
1. 燒鴨去除鴨骨後，將肉切成細絲；竹笙泡脹開來，洗淨、切粗絲；香菇泡軟與煮熟之筍分別切細絲；香菜切段。
2. 鍋內燒2大匙油先將蔥、薑爆香，待蔥薑焦黃後，淋下酒，同時注入清湯，將蔥薑揀出不要，加入醬油使湯成茶色，再放入各項材料煮滾（香菜除外）。
3. 酌量加入鹽調味後，用太白粉水勾芡，淋下少許麻油便可裝碗，再撒上香菜。

   ＊這道菜亦可將高湯的份量加多，而成為一道湯菜。

   ＊**You may add more soup stock to make this dish as a soup.**

Ingredients：
150g. roasted duck, 4 pieces bamboo mushroom, 2 black mushrooms, 1 bamboo shoot, 1T. shredded ham, 1stalk green onion, 2 slices ginger, 2½C. soup stock, 2 stalks coriander

Seasonings：
2T. soy sauce, 2T. wine, 2t. salt, sesame oil, 1½ T. cornstarch paste

Procedures：
1. Remove the bones, and shred the roasted duck ; soak the bamboo mushrooms to soft, cut into stripes ; soak the black mushrooms until soft. Cook the bamboo shoot. Shred both. Trim the coriander and cut into sections.
2. Heat 2T. oil to fry green onions and gingers until brown. Sprinkle with 1T. wine. Add soup stock. Remove green onion and ginger. Add soy sauce and all the shredded ingredients (except the coriander). Bring to a boil.
3. Season with salt. Thicken with cornstarch paste. Drop a little sesame oil and remove. Sprinkle coriander.

袈裟牛肉
Deep-fried Beef Sandwich

材料：
絞牛肉6兩、絞肥肉1兩、蔥屑2大匙、
豆腐衣4張

調味料：
蛋白1個、薑汁½茶匙、清水2大匙、酒1大匙、醬油1大匙、
鹽⅓茶匙、雞粉少許、胡椒粉少許

做法：

1. 絞牛肉盛大碗中，加入絞肥肉、蔥屑、薑汁及調味料，用多支竹筷順同一方向攪拌，至十分有黏性。
2. 豆腐衣修切成長方形15×30公分，在靠手邊4公分的地方攤放¼量的牛肉（約2兩）成一扁長條，並向前方捲疊，封口處用少許蛋白黏住。
3. 將牛肉條切成4公分寬之斜段（即成菱角形），投入7分熱的炸油中，大火炸成金黃而外皮酥脆狀。撈出裝盤，附上花椒鹽與番茄醬上桌即可。

＊乾鍋中小火炒香1大匙花椒粉（約10秒），再加入3大匙鹽炒一下即為花椒鹽。

＊ **Stir-fry 1T. brown peppercorn powder in a pan over low heat for 10 seconds, add 3T. salt. Stir-fry for a few seconds longer. Remove. This is brown peppercorn salt.**

Ingredients:
250g. ground beef, 40g. ground pork fat,
2T. chopped green onion,
4 pieces dried soybean sheet,
brown peppercorn salt or ketchup

Seasonings:
2T. egg white, 1/2t. ginger juice, 2T. water, 1T. wine,
1T. soy sauce, 1/3t. salt, a pinch of pepper

Procedures:

1. Place ground beef and ground pork fat in a large bowl. Add green onion, ginger juice, and the seasonings. Stir in one direction until the meat is very sticky.
2. Cut the dried soybean sheets into pieces 15cm wide × 30cm long. Place 4cm wide of the beef mixture across the lower part of the sheet, shaping it about 4cm wide. Fold over twice into a flat roll. Seal the edge and ends with a little of egg white. Make all 4 beef rolls.
3. Cut the rolls into pieces 4cm wide wine. Deep-fry in hot oil until the outside becomes golden brown and crispy. Remove to platter. Serve with brown peppercorn salt or ketchup.

牛羊類

牛羊類

五彩牛柳
Five - Colored Beef Strips

材料：

嫩牛肉4兩、青椒絲1/2杯、熟胡蘿蔔絲1/4杯、酸菜絲1/4杯、綠豆芽2兩、洋蔥絲1/2杯、嫩薑絲2大匙

調味料：

（1）醬油1大匙、太白粉1大匙、嫩精（或小蘇打）1/4茶匙、水2大匙
（2）鹽1/3茶匙、糖1/4茶匙、水2大匙

做法：

1. 選牛肉時應選顏色鮮紅、而纖維較細之嫩牛肉，逆絲切成如筷子般粗細，4公分長之條狀，用調味料（1）拌勻，醃30分鐘以上。
2. 將鍋燒熱後放1杯的油，待油熱至八分熱時，放下牛肉，大火將牛肉快速泡熟、撈出，瀝乾油汁。
3. 另熱2大匙油，先將洋蔥絲炒軟，加入薑絲、酸菜絲（應選用菜心較嫩之部分）、胡蘿蔔、青椒絲及豆芽，大火快炒10秒鐘後，加調味料（2）和牛肉，拌炒均勻便可裝盤上桌。

Ingredients：

150g. beef tenderloin, 1/4C. shredded green pepper, 1/4C. cooked carrot, shredded, 1/4C. shredded pickled mustard, 80g. bean sprouts, 1/2C. shredded onion

Seasonings：

（1）1T. soy sauce, 1T. cornstarch, 1/4t. meat tenderizer or baking soda, 2T. water
（2）1/3t. salt, 1/4t. sugar, 2T. water

Procedures：

1. Cut the beef across the grain into strings 0.8cm wide×4cm long. Marinate with seasonings (1) for 30 minutes.
2. Heat 2C. oil to 160°C. Stir-fry beef strings over high heat for about 15 seconds. Drain.
3. Heat 2T. oil to stir-fry shredded onion, when onion becomes soft, and shredded ginger, pickled mustard, carrot, green pepper, and bean sprouts. Stir-fry over high heat for 10 seconds. Add seasonings (2), place beef in, mix thoroughly. Transfer to serving platter.

＊平時炒牛肉的基本方法亦與此相同，可將五種配料簡化成一、二種亦較方便。

＊**This is the basic method for stir-frying beef. You may choose any kind and quantity of vegetable to stir-fry with the beef.**

麻辣牛肉
Sliced Beef with Chili Sauce

材料：
滷牛腱4兩、粉皮1疊、萵苣筍1/2支

調味料：
蔥花1大匙、花椒粉1/2茶匙、大蒜泥1茶匙、糖1/2茶匙、醬油2大匙、鎮江醋1/2大匙、麻油1大匙、辣油1大匙

做法：
1. 牛腱切成極薄的片狀，盛在有洞的漏勺內，放入開水中燙約3秒鐘、瀝乾。
2. 粉皮切條狀（也可用素雞切片代替粉皮），洗淨、瀝乾；萵苣筍切片，用少許鹽抓拌，醃5分鐘，擠乾水分。三種材料排放盤中。
3. 在一只碗中，將調味料拌勻，上桌後淋在牛肉片上，仔細拌勻即好。

＊如買不到滷牛腱，可買生的牛腱子，先整個用滾水燙過後，放在鍋內加入蔥、薑、八角、醬油、酒及滾水，用大火滷50～60分鐘，待湯汁冷後，取出使用即可。

Ingredients：
150g. braised beef, 1piece mung bean sheet, 1/2 green bamboo shoot

Seasonings：
1T. chopped green onion, 1/2t. brown peppercorn powder, 1t. mashed garlic, 1/2t. sugar, 2T. soy sauce, 1/2T. vinegar, 1T. sesame oil, 1T. red chili oil

Procedures：
1. Slices the braised beef, place in a strainer and blanch for 3 seconds. Drain.
2. Cut the mung bean sheet into strips 1 1/2cm wide. Rinse and drain it dry. Slice green bamboo shoot, marinate with some salt for 5 minutes, squeeze dry. Arrange 3 kinds of ingredients in a plate.
3. Mix the seasonings in a bowl. Serve with the beef. Mix well before eating.

＊**To make braised beef：boil the raw beef in water for 2 minutes. Cook the beef with green onion, ginger, star anise, soy sauce, wine, and 4C. hot water. Cook for 50~60 minutes.**

白灼牛肉片

Poached Beef Slices, Hong Kong Style

材料：

嫩牛肉6兩、綠豆芽6兩、蔥絲3大匙、嫩薑絲2大匙、紅辣椒絲1大匙、香菜2大匙

調味料：

（1）鹽1/4茶匙、太白粉1大匙、水2大匙
（2）醬油1大匙、清湯2大匙、麻油少許、鹽1/2茶匙

做法：

1. 牛肉洗淨後，逆絲切成3公分四方大小的片狀，泡在清水中抓洗，使血水流出，而肉色呈白淨。撈出、瀝得極乾後，再用調味料（1）抓拌，醃10分鐘左右。
2. 蔥、薑、紅辣椒及香菜切絲後拌勻，一半放在盤子的一端，另一半放在小碗中，與調味料（2）料混合。
3. 將綠豆芽摘去頭尾，只留中段部分（稱為銀芽），在鍋中用2大匙油，大火快炒，加少許鹽調味，盛出、瀝乾油汁後，裝在盤中做為墊底用。
4. 在鍋中將3杯水煮滾（如有上湯則更佳），水中加入油1大匙，待水再滾時，將牛肉放下，以大火灼燙大約10秒鐘，即刻撈出，瀝乾後，放在豆芽上，與小碗中之沾牛肉料一同上桌，供沾食用。

Ingredients：

250g. beef tenderloin, 150g. bean sports, 3T. shredded green onion, 2T. shredded ginger, 1T. shredded red chili, 2T. coriander

Seasonings：

（1）1/4t. salt, 1T. cornstarch, 2T. water
（2）1T. soy sauce, 2T. soup stock, 1/4t. sesame oil, 1t. salt

Procedures：

1. Slice the beef across the grain into 3cm squares. Rinse in water, stirring the beef so the blood will rinse away and the color of the beef becomes lighter. Drain and marinate with seasonings (1) for 10 minutes.
2. Mix the green onion, ginger, red chili, and coriander together in a bowl. Place half of the amount on one side of the platter, and mix the other half with the sauce.
3. Trim the bean sprouts. Stir-fry with 2T. oil over high heat. Add a little salt, then drain. Place on the plate.
4. Add 1T. oil to 3C. boiling water (you may use soup stock). Add the beef, boil over high heat for 10 seconds. Drain the beef and place on top of the bean sprouts. Serve with the sauce.

咖哩燒牛腩
Braised Beef with Curry Sauce

材料：
牛腩或肋條1斤、蔥2支、薑2片、馬鈴薯1個、胡蘿蔔½支、咖哩粉2大匙、大蒜屑1大匙

調味料：
酒2大匙、鹽1茶匙、糖¼茶匙

做法：
1. 牛腩整塊投入約5杯的開水中，加蔥、薑、酒，以小火煮半小時。取出牛腩，待稍涼後，切成3公分寬，4公分長之厚片狀。
2. 馬鈴薯及胡蘿蔔切成與牛肉相同大小的滾刀塊備用。
3. 鍋中燒熱3大匙油，先將大蒜屑爆香，再用小火慢慢將咖哩粉炒香，將牛肉加入同炒片刻後，注入煮牛肉剩下之湯汁，再繼續煮上40~50分鐘左右。
4. 用鹽和糖調味後，加入馬鈴薯及胡蘿蔔，再續煮半小時至牛腩已夠爛，並開大火將湯汁略加收乾，即可裝盤。

Ingredients：
600g. beef brisket, 2 stalks green onion, 2 slices ginger, 1 potatoe, ½ carrot, 2T. curry powder, 1T. chopped garlic

Seasonings：
2T. wine, 1T. salt, ¼t. sugar

Procedures:
1. Cook the whole beef brisket in 5C. boiling water. Add green onion, ginger, and wine. Simmer for ½ hour. Remove the beef and let it cool. Reserve the broth. Cut beef into pieces 3cm×4cm.
2. Cut the potato and carrot into pieces, the same size as the beef.
3. Heat 3 T. oil to fry the garlic. Add the curry powder and stir-fry over low heat. Place the beef in, stir-fry for 1 minute. Add the broth. Simmer for another 40~50 minutes.
4. Season with salt and sugar. Add potato and carrot. Simmer for ½ hour until the beef is tender. Reduce the broth to ½ C. over high heat. Remove to platter.

✽ 如想用此咖哩牛肉之汁拌飯時，則應多加水分同煮，最後剩下之汁，則用少許太白粉勾芡，以使湯汁濃稠，適宜拌飯用。

✽ If you want to put the curry sauce over rice, you may add more water when you cooking the beef. Use some cornstarch paste to thicken the sauce.

蔥薑焗牛肉
Beef with Green Onion and Ginger

材料：
嫩牛肉6兩、芥藍菜半斤、蔥5支、薑10片

調味料：
(1) 醬油1/2大匙、太白粉1大匙、小蘇打粉1/4茶匙、水2~3大匙
(2) 醬油1/2大匙、蠔油1大匙、糖1/4茶匙、胡椒粉少許、水4大匙

做法：
1. 牛肉切薄片，用調味料（1）拌勻，至少醃30分鐘。
2. 蔥切約5公分長段；芥藍菜摘好、燙過、過冷水後放在砂鍋中，用小火將砂鍋燒熱。
3. 將1/2杯油燒至九分熱，放下牛肉過油炒一下，約八分熟即盛出。
4. 放下蔥段、薑片炒至香且黃，放下牛肉再拌炒一下，淋下調味料（2），再全部澆在芥藍菜上，蓋上砂鍋蓋，大火燒至開即可。

Ingredients:
250g. beef tenderloin, 300g. Chinese kale, 5 stalks green onion, 10 slices ginger

Seasonings:
(1) 1/2T. soy sauce, 1T. cornstarch, 1/4t. baking soda, 2~3T. water
(2) 1/2T. soy sauce, 1T. oyster sauce, 1/4t. sugar, a pinch of pepper, 4T. water

Procedures:
1. Slice the beef, marinate with seasonings (1) for 30 minutes.
2. Cut green onion into 5cm long；trim the Chinese kale, blanch and rinse until cold. Drain and place it in a casserole dish, heat the casserole dish over low heat.
3. Heat 1/2C. oil to 180°C, Stir-fry beef over high heat until the beef is almost done, remove.
4. Stir-fry green onion and ginger, fry until brown, add beef in, stir evenly, pour the seasonings (2) in, and remove all into the casserole dish. Cover and bring to a boil over high heat. Serve hot.

牛羊類

漢堡牛肉餅
Home Style Hamburgers

材料：
絞牛肉半斤、洋蔥屑1/2杯、奶油1大匙、土司麵包1片、牛奶1/2杯、蛋1個、馬鈴薯、胡蘿蔔、洋芹各適量

調味料：
鹽1茶匙、胡椒粉少許、紅酒1大匙、清湯或水1/2杯、太白粉水少許

做法：

1. 洋蔥屑用奶油和1大匙油混合炒香且軟，盛入大碗中。土司麵包去硬邊，撕成小片，也放碗中，加牛奶拌勻。
2. 約2~3分鐘後，加入牛肉、蛋、鹽和胡椒粉，抓拌均勻，摔打數下，分成4份。
3. 平底鍋中燒熱3大匙油，將每份牛肉分別做成肉餅狀，放入油中大火煎半分鐘，翻面再煎約1分鐘至黃，改小火煎熟。肉餅太厚時可以撒少許水，蓋上鍋蓋燜一下，較容易熟。
4. 肉餅盛出，淋下紅酒到鍋中餘汁內，加清湯煮滾，再以鹽調味，勾薄芡後淋在肉餅上。附上炸馬鈴薯和炒過的胡蘿蔔和西芹（配菜可自行搭配）。

Ingredients：
300g. ground beef, 1/2C. chopped onion, 1T. butter, 1piece bread, 1/2C. milk, 1 egg, potato, carrot, celery

Seasonings：
1t. salt, a pinch of pepper, 1T. red wine, 1/2C. soup stock or water, a little of cornstarch

Procedures：

1. Stir-fry chopped onion with butter and 1T. oil until fragrant, remove to a bowl. Remove bread crust, cut into small pieces, place in the bowl, add milk in.
2. Soak for 2~3 minutes, add beef, egg, salt and pepper in, mix thoroughly. Divide into 4 parts.
3. Heat 3T. oil in a frying pan. Make the beef mixture into a hamburger, fry over high heat for 1/2 minute, turn it over and fry for another minute until the both sides get brown. Turn to low heat, fry until done. Sprinkle some water into the pan, cover and simmer for a while to make the hamburger done, if the hamburgers are too thick.
4. Remove hamburgers to serving plate. Pour red wine to pan, add soup stock, bring to a boil, season with some salt, thicken with cornstarch paste, pour over hamburgers. Serve with fried potato, stir-fried carrot and celery.

鮮茄牛腩
Stewed Beef with Tomato

材料：
牛腩1斤、洋蔥1個、蕃茄2個、薑3片、大蒜6粒

調味料：
酒2大匙、醬油5大匙、糖2茶匙、開水4杯、
番茄膏（糊）2大匙

做法：

1. 牛腩或牛肋條切成3公分四方塊後，全部在開水中川燙30秒撈出。
2. 洋蔥切約1公分之寬條；番茄去皮、切成塊狀；大蒜拍碎。
3. 鍋中燒熱2大匙油後，先放下大蒜及薑片爆香，再放進洋蔥慢慢炒至洋蔥變軟。
4. 再放下番茄及牛肉同炒片刻，淋下酒、醬油，加糖及開水，大火煮滾後，改用小火慢慢燒至牛肉夠爛為止。（喜歡番茄者可在最後再加1個番茄同煮。）
5. 用油2大匙將番茄膏炒至紅亮，加入牛肉中同燒一下便可裝盤。

Ingredients：
600g. beef brisket, 1 onion, 2 tomatoes, 3slices ginger, 6 garlic cloves

Seasonings：
2T. wine, 5T. soy sauce, 2t. sugar, 4C. hot water, 2T. tomato paste

Procedures:

1. Cut the beef into 3cm cubes. Boil in water for 30 seconds. Drain.
2. Shred the onion into 1cm strips；Remove the skin from the tomatoes, cut into cubes；crush the garlic cloves.
3. Heat 2T. oil to fry the garlic and ginger; add onion, stir-fry over low heat until the onion becomes soft.
4. Add tomatoes and beef. Stir-fry again. Add wine, soy sauce, sugar, and hot water. Bring to a boil, then simmer for $1^{1/2}$ hours until the beef is tender. (You may add another tomato at last if you like the taste of tomato.)
5. Stir-fry tomato paste with 2T. oil. When it becomes shiny, add it to the beef. Cook for a while, then remove.

蔥爆羊肉
Sautéed Lamb with Scallion

材料：
火鍋羊肉片（前腿肉或後腿肉）半斤、大蒜片3大匙、蔥絲2杯

調味料：
（1）醬油1大匙、花椒粉1/4茶匙、酒1/2大匙、油1大匙
（2）醬油1大匙、醋1/2大匙、麻油1/2茶匙

做法：
1. 將調味料（1）在大碗內混合，放下羊肉片仔細拌勻，醃上10分鐘左右。
2. 將調味料（2）先調好備用。
3. 炒鍋燒熱後，由鍋邊淋下油4大匙，再將油燒得冒煙，落大蒜片及羊肉片下鍋，用大火快加翻炒，約炒5秒鐘後放下蔥絲，再快拌炒5秒鐘左右。
4. 淋下調味料（2），大火快加鏟拌均勻，見肉已全熟，即可熄火、馬上裝盤供食。

Ingredients:
300g. sliced lean lamb, 3T. garlic slices,
2C. shredded green onion

Seasonings:
（1） 1T. soy sauce, 1/4t. salt, 1/4t. brown peppercorn pepper, 1/2T. wine, 1T. oil
（2） 1T. soy sauce, 1/2T. vinegar, 1/2t. sesame oil

Procedure:
1. Mix the seasonings (1) in a bowl, marinate the lamb for 10 minutes.
2. Prepare the seasonings (2) in a small bowl.
3. Heat 4T. oil in the wok until very hot. Add sliced garlic and lamb, stir-fry quickly over high heat for 5 seconds. Add shredded green onion and stir-fry for another 5 seconds.
4. Sprinkle the seasonings (2), continuing to stir-fry until thoroughly heated. Serve immediately.

牛羊類

牛羊類

砂鍋羊肉
Stewed Lamb in Casserole Dish

材料：
羊腿肉1斤、大蒜5粒、蔥2支、白蘿蔔1/2斤、高麗菜12兩、凍豆腐1塊、寬粉絲1把、青蒜1支

調味料：
醬油2/3杯、酒2大匙、八角1顆、糖1茶匙、鹽酌量

做法：
1. 將羊肉連皮切成6公分四方的厚片，全部用開水燙煮1分鐘後撈出，沖過冷水、瀝乾。
2. 鍋中燒熱油3大匙爆香大蒜及蔥段，放下羊肉同炒，淋下酒及醬油，放入八角、糖及切塊的白蘿蔔，注入水（水要超過羊肉3公分），大火煮滾後，改小火燒煮1小時。
3. 將煮好的羊肉移入砂鍋中，羊肉湯中之白蘿蔔等揀出不要，羊肉湯倒進砂鍋中（湯如果不夠，此時可再加開水），加入切塊的凍豆腐、高麗菜，再以小火燉煮10分鐘。
4. 將泡軟之寬粉絲放入羊肉鍋中煮至夠軟，用鹽調味並撒下青蒜絲便可上桌。

Ingredients：
600g. lamb (leg portion), 5 garlic cloves, 2stalks green onion 300g. radish, 450g. cabbage, 1piece frozen bean curd, 1bundle mung bean threads, 1 green garlic

Seasonings：
2/3C. soy sauce, 2T. wine, 1 star anise, 1t. sugar, salt

Procedures：
1. Cut the lamb into thick pieces (about 6cm thick) with the skin. Boil for 1 minute. Drain and rinse with water.
2. Heat 3T. oil to fry garlic cloves and green onion. Add lamb, sprinkle with wine and soy sauce. Add star anise, sugar, radish cubes, and water (the water must cover the lamb). Bring to a boil, then simmer for1 hour.
3. Transfer lamb and soup to a casserole dish. (drain the soup and the soup should cover the lamb; if it does not, add more water). Add frozen bean curd and cabbage in, cook over low heat for 10 minutes.
4. Place soaked bean threads in, cook until soft, season with salt. Sprinkle the shredded green garlic at last. Serve.

* 羊肉性熱，宜冬季食用，砂鍋可以保暖。
* **This dish is good for winter.**

海鮮類

脆底蝦仁
Stir-fried Shrimp with Yu-tiau

材料：
蝦仁6兩、油條2支、蔥段15小段、薑片10小片

調味料：
（1）蛋白1大匙、鹽1/4茶匙、太白粉1茶匙
（2）酒1/2大匙、鹽1/4茶匙、麻油1/4茶匙、太白粉1/4茶匙、水3大匙

做法：
1. 蝦剝殼、抽去腸砂後，加入1/2茶匙鹽，以手指加以抓捏，全部放在一個大盆中，用自來水不斷沖洗。一面沖，一面攪動，以使蝦仁之黏液完全洗淨，撈出、瀝乾水分，再用乾紙巾或布，將水分完全吸乾。
2. 在碗中將調味料（1）調勻，放入蝦仁仔細拌勻。放進冰箱中醃20分鐘以上。
3. 油條切成小薄片後，放入烤箱中烤脆，或放入熱油中，炸至金黃而酥脆時撈出，攤在一張紙上吸去油，堆放在盤中墊底。
4. 鍋子先燒熱後，放入油1杯，再燒至八分熱，放下蝦仁，大火過油約15秒鐘，見蝦仁變白即撈出，將油倒出。
5. 在鍋中燒熱2大匙油，先爆香蔥段和薑片，再將蝦仁倒回鍋中，淋下調味料（2），大火拌炒均勻，便可盛出，裝在油條上即好。

Ingredients：
250g. shrimp (shelled), 2 pieces yu-tiau, 15 green onion sections, 10 slices ginger

Seasonings：
（1）1T. egg white, 1/4t. salt, 1t. cornstarch
（2）1/2T. wine, 1/4t. salt, 1/4t. sesame oil, 1/4t. cornstarch, 3T. water

Procedures:
1. Remove the black vein from the shrimp, clean with 1/2t. salt thoroughly. Place the shrimp in a large bowl and rinse with large amount of water. Drain and pat it dry with paper towel.
2. Mix seasonings (1) in a bowl, add shrimp in, mix thoroughly. Place in refrigerator for at least 20 minutes.
3. Dice the Yu-T'iau and deep-fry in hot oil until golden brown and crispy. Drain and place on a plate. (You may bake the yu-tiau in oven until crispy).
4. Heat 1C. oil to about 160°C. Add shrimp, stir-fry over high heat for about 15 seconds, when the color changed, drain.
5. Heat 2T. oil to fry green onions and ginger, return shrimp, add seasonings (2), stir-fry over high heat, mix thoroughly. Place on top of yu-tiau and serve.

＊也可將墊底的油條改為炸米粉或粉絲、切片之餛飩皮、玉米片等料，只要可炸得酥脆的材料均可應用。

＊Instead of yu-tiau, you may deep-fry rice noodles, bean threads, diced won-ton skins or any other ingredient which will become crispy when fried.

海鮮類

茄汁蝦仁
Stir-fried Shrimp with Ketchup

材料：
蝦仁6兩、蔥屑1大匙、蒜屑1/2大匙、青菜1/2斤

調味料：
(1) 蛋白1大匙、太白粉2茶匙、鹽1/3茶匙
(2) 鹽1/3茶匙、番茄醬1 1/2大匙、酒1/2大匙、
　　鹽1/4茶匙、麻油少許

做法：
1. 蝦仁的處理方法請參考67頁之「脆底蝦仁」。碗中將調味料（1）調勻，放下蝦仁拌勻，放入冰箱中，醃20分鐘以上。
2. 選購豆苗、青花菜或西洋菜等綠色青菜，摘成適當大小，用油炒熟、加鹽調味，盛出。瀝乾水分放在盤中，做墊底或圍飾之用。
3. 油1杯燒至八分熱時，將蝦仁放入過油，大火炒約15秒鐘便可撈出，將油倒出僅留2大匙左右，先爆香蔥、蒜屑，再放下調味料（2）炒香，落蝦仁迅速拌炒勻合，盛出放在青菜上。

Ingredients：
250g. shrimp (shelled), 1T. chopped green onion, 1/2T. chopped garlic, 300g. green vegetable

Seasonings：
(1) 1T. egg white, 2t. cornstarch, 1/3t. salt
(2) 1/3t. salt, 1 1/2T. ketchup, 1/2T. wine, 1/4t. salt, a fewdrops of sesame oil

Procedures：
1. Refer to the recipe of page 67 about how to clean the shrimp. Mix seasonings (1) to marinate shrimp for 20 minutes in the refrigerator.
2. Choose any kind of green vegetable. Trim and stir-fry it, season with salt, remove to the plate.
3. Heat 1C. oil to 160°C. Fry the shrimp for about 15 seconds. Drain. Use only 2T. oil to stir-fry the green onion and garlic. Add seasonings (2) and shrimp, stir-fry thoroughly. Remove to platter. Serve with the vegetable.

蒜茸蒸草蝦
Steamed Prawns with Garlic Sauce

材料：
草蝦8隻、大蒜泥3大匙、蔥粒3大匙

調味料：
鹽1/3茶匙、酒1/2大匙、上好醬油2大匙、水2大匙、胡椒粉少許

做法：
1. 草蝦每隻剪下鬚及前腳後，由背部對剖開，將切口朝上排在盤內，撒下鹽和用水3大匙調開的大蒜泥，並淋下酒。
2. 待鍋中之水已沸滾時，將蝦放入，用大火蒸5分鐘。
3. 取出蝦，撒下蔥粒及胡椒粉。小鍋內燒熱1大匙油，淋下調勻的醬油和水，趁其煮滾時，馬上澆到蝦上面，再用湯匙來回舀起盤內之醬油汁、淋到蝦上數次即可上桌。

Ingredients:
8 prawns, 3T. mashed garlic, 3T. chopped green onion

Seasonings:
1/3t. salt, 1/2T. wine, 2T. soy sauce, 2T. water, pepper

Procedures:
1. Trim the prawns and split from the back to make the prawn lie flat. Arrange on a platter. Sprinkle salt, garlic juice (mix 3T. water with 3T. smashed garlic), and wine over the top.
2. Steam the prawns over high heat for 5 minutes.
3. Remove the prawns. Sprinkle with chopped green onion and pepper. Heat 1T. oil, pour the soy sauce and water in, pour over the prawns. Spoon the sauce several times over the prawns before serving.

海鮮類

海鮮類

70

乾燒明蝦段
Sautéed Prawns with Hot Sauce

材料：
明蝦4隻、洋蔥1個、蔥屑2大匙、薑屑½大匙

調味料：
番茄醬2大匙、辣椒油½大匙、酒1大匙、鹽½茶匙、糖½茶匙、水1杯、太白粉水2茶匙、麻油¼茶匙

做法：

1. 明蝦抽去腸砂後，剪去頭尖及尾尖部分，並將蝦腳修齊，洗淨後視大小將每隻切為二或三段。
2. 洋蔥切絲，用2大匙油炒香熟且軟，加鹽少許調味，盛入盤中墊底。
3. 燒熱4大匙油，放下全部明蝦，用大火將蝦兩面均煎過，至全部變成紅色，用漏勺瀝出。
4. 用鍋中剩餘之油來爆炒蔥、薑屑，並加入番茄醬拌炒，見已夠紅亮時，淋下酒、鹽及糖，注入1杯清水和明蝦，小火燒約2~3分鐘，淋下太白粉水勾芡，淋下辣椒油及麻油，拌勻盛到洋蔥上，便可上桌。

Ingredients：
4 prawns, 1 onion, 2T. chopped green onion, 1T. chopped ginger

Seasonings：
2T. ketchup, ½T. chili oil, 1T. wine, ½t. salt, ½t. sugar, 1C. water, 2t. cornstarch paste, ¼t. sesame oil

Procedures：

1. Remove black vein from the prawns. Cut off the sharp part of the head and the feet. Cut into 2 or 3 pieces per prawn, depending on the size.
2. Stir-fry shredded onion with 2T. oil until soft. Season with a little of salt. Drain excess liquid. Remove to a platter.
3. Heat 4T. oil, add the prawns. Fry both sides over high heat. When the prawns turn red, remove immediately.
4. Stir-fry chopped green onion and ginger with the remaining oil, add ketchup, stir-fry again. When ketchup becomes shiny, add wine, salt, sugar, and water. Return prawns to the wok. Simmer for 2~3 minutes. Thicken with cornstarch paste. Sprinkle with chili oil and sesame oil. Mix thoroughly and serve.

＊同樣口味可以燒小蝦子或蝦仁。

＊**You may sauteed shrimp or shelled shrimp with the same way.**

海鮮類

72

碧綠琵琶蝦
Steamed Prawns

材料：
草蝦6隻、餛飩皮（薄的）6張、香菜葉6枚、蝦仁3兩、絞豬肥肉1兩

調味料：
（1）鹽1/4茶匙、酒1茶匙
（2）蛋白1大匙、鹽、胡椒粉各少許、酒1茶匙、麻油1/4茶匙、太白粉1大匙

做法：
1. 草蝦摘下頭、剝除殼（僅留下尾殼），由背部切入刀口，抽出腸砂，並抽斷腹筋，攤平蝦肉成一大片，撒下調味料（1）。
2. 蝦仁剁爛、加入調味料（2），順同一方向攪拌至有黏性為止。
3. 將蝦仁料1大匙做成蛋形，放在塗了油的碟上，並將1隻草蝦正面向下、覆蓋在上面。放上一枚香菜葉，蓋上一張餛飩皮。
4. 全部做好之後，上鍋大火蒸12分鐘（鍋中先將水燒滾才蒸）。取出趁熱送食。

Ingredients：
6 prawns, 6 pieces won-ton skin, 6 parsley leaves, 120g. shrimp, 40g. ground pork fat

Seasonings：
（1） 1/4t. salt, 1t. wine
（2） 1 egg white, 1t. wine, 1/4t. sesame oil, 1T. cornstarch, salt & pepper

Procedures：
1. Shell prawns but keep the tail shell. Remove the black vein of the prawns and cut off the white vein from the bottom (or the prawns will curl). Split each prawn lengthwise down the back, but don't serve it. The prawns should lie flat, sprinkle seasonings (1) on prawns.
2. Smash the shrimp, mix with the seasonings (2).
3. Use 1T. of shrimp mixture to make an egg-shaped cake, arrange on a greased plate. Place a prawn on top of the cake then put a parsley leave on top of the prawn. Cover with a won-ton skin. Make all ten prawns.
4. Steam the prawns over high heat for 12 minutes. Remove and serve hot.

海鮮類

西蘭鳳尾蝦
Stir-fried Prawns with Broccoli

材料：
小型草蝦12隻或蘆蝦20隻、青花菜1小個、蔥段10小段、薑片10片

調味料：
（1）鹽1/4茶匙、酒1茶匙、蛋白1大匙、太白粉2茶匙
（2）酒1/2大匙、水4大匙、太白粉1/4茶匙、鹽1/2茶匙、麻油數滴

做法：
1. 選用較小之草蝦（或較大之蘆蝦均可），剝殼、但留下尾部一截，抽去腸砂，在背部劃切很深之刀口。全部放在大碗內，用半茶匙的鹽輕輕抓洗，沖過多量的清水後，用乾布或紙巾將水分完全吸乾。
2. 將調味料（1）在碗中調勻（蛋白須打散），放入蝦片醃20分鐘左右。
3. 青花菜除去外皮，分成一朵朵，全部在開水中燙熟，撈出後用冷水沖涼備用。
4. 鍋中將1杯油燒至九分熱，倒下蝦片，大火快炒至蝦肉已轉白、且彎曲成球狀便可瀝出。
5. 另用2大匙油將蔥段、薑片爆香，放下青花菜略炒，再倒下蝦球及調味料（2），大火迅速拌勻、起鍋，裝入盤中。

Ingredients：
12 small prawns, 1 broccoli, 10 green onion sections, 10 slices ginger

Seasonings：
（1） 1/4t. salt, 1t. wine, 1T. egg white, 2t. cornstarch
（2） 1/2T. wine, 4T. water, 1/4t. cornstarch, 1/4t. salt, a few drops of sesame oil

Procedures：
1. Choose the smaller prawns or larger shrimp. Shell the prawns, but keep the tail shell, remove the black vein. Make a deep cut on the back of each prawn lengthwise, but don't sever it. Place in a large bowl, add 1/2t. salt to clean the prawns. Rinse with a large amount of water. Drain and pat it dry with paper towel.
2. Beat the egg white. Mix the seasonings (1), marinate the prawns for 20 minutes.
3. Trim the broccoli into pieces. Boil, then rinse with cold water. Drain.
4. Heat 1C. oil to 180°C. Add the prawns and quickly stir-fry over high heat until the prawns become light and curly.
5. Stir-fry the green onion and ginger with 1T. oil. Add broccoli and stir-fry for a few seconds. Then add the prawns and seasonings (2). Mix thoroughly over high heat. Transfer to a serving platter.

＊廣東人稱青花菜為西蘭花，故名之。

海鮮類

76

生炒蝦鬆

Stir-fried Minced Shrimp

材料：

蝦仁6兩、香菇或洋菇屑1/3杯、筍片1/3杯、青豆2大匙、蛋皮丁半杯、韭黃丁1/3杯、乾米粉1兩、生菜葉12片

調味料：

（1）鹽1/4茶匙、太白粉1/2茶匙、蛋白1大匙
（2）淡色醬油1/2大匙、鹽1/3茶匙、太白粉2茶匙、清湯或水3大匙、胡椒粉少許、麻油少許

做法：

1. 蝦仁抽去腸砂後，用1/2茶匙的鹽抓洗，沖淨並用紙巾擦乾水分，每隻都切成小丁，用調味料（1）拌醃10分鐘。
2. 米粉用熱油、大火炸至泡起（約6秒鐘），撈出，瀝乾油後壓碎，堆放在盤中。
3. 在炒鍋內將油1/2杯燒至味八分熱，放下蝦仁大火炒熟，瀝出備用。
4. 用2大匙油炒香香菇、筍片、青豆、蛋皮等配料，並再傾入蝦仁丁及調味料（2），大火快速拌炒均勻，最後加入韭黃丁一拌便起鍋，盛在米粉上，附上生菜葉一起上桌包食。

Ingredients：

250g. shelled shrimp, 1/3C. chopped black mushroom (or mushrooms), 1/3C. diced bamboo shoot, 2T. green peas, 1/2C. diced egg pancake, 1/3C. diced white leek, 40g. dried rice noodle, 12 pieces lettuce leaves

Seasonings：

(1) 1/4 t. salt, 1/2t. cornstarch, 1T. egg white
(2) 1/2T. light colored soy sauce, 1/3t. salt, 2t. cornstarch, 3T. soup stock or water, pepper and sesame oil

Procedures：

1. Remove the black vein from the shrimp. Rub with salt, then rinse with water. Pat it dry. Cut each shrimp into small cubes. Marinate with seasonings (1) for 10 minutes.
2. Deep-fry the rice noodles in hot oil for 6 seconds. Drain and place on a platter. Crush slightly.
3. Heat 1/2C. oil to 160°C. Add the shrimp, stir-fry over high heat until done. Drain.
4. Stir-fry black mushrooms, bamboo shoots, green peas, and diced egg together with 2T. oil. Add the shrimp and seasonings (2). Stir-fry thoroughly. Add diced white leeks. Turn off the heat. Mix and remove to the platter on top of the rice noodles. Serve with lettuce leaves. Wrap shrimp mixture in a piece of lettuce leave, and eat.

炒蔭豉蚵
Stir-fried Oysters

材料：
新鮮生蚵6兩、豆豉2大匙、大蒜屑1大匙、紅辣椒段1大匙、青蒜段3大匙

調味料：
鹽1/2茶匙、酒1/2大匙、醬油膏1 1/2大匙、糖1/4茶匙、胡椒粉少許、太白粉水適量

做法：
1. 將1/2茶匙鹽撒在蚵上面，用手指輕輕捏洗一下，摘下硬殼、沖過清水、瀝乾。
2. 將生蚵放入3杯冷水中，開火加熱，當水將要沸滾時，關火、瀝出蚵。
3. 起油鍋，用2大匙油爆香豆豉及大蒜屑，加入酒等調味料，並放下蚵，用大火炒5秒鐘。
4. 放下青蒜段和紅椒丁，再勾一點薄芡。熄火後馬上盛在碟中送食。

Ingredients：
250g. oyster, 2T. fermented black beans, 1T. chopped garlic, 1T. red chili sections, 3T. green garlic sections

Seasonings：
1/2t. salt, 1/2T. wine, 1 1/2T. soy sauce paste, 1/4t. sugar, pepper, cornstarch paste

Procedures:
1. Rub the oysters gently with salt. Rinse with water. Drain.
2. Put the oyster in a pot with 3C. cold water, turn on the heat to heat it up. Turn off the heat just before the water is boiling, remove the oyster quickly.
3. Heat 2T. oil to stir-fry the fermented black beans and garlic over low heat for 10 seconds. Add wine, soy sauce paste, sugar, pepper and oyster. Stir-fry over high heat for 5 seconds.
4. Add green garlic and red chili, thicken with cornstarch paste. Remove and serve hot.

* 生蚵很容易收縮，不可炒得太久，也必須盡速取食。

* Use only small oysters in stir-fry dishes, the large oysters are not suitable. Oysters shrink very fast when cooked. Be careful not to stir-fry it too long. Oysters must be eaten as soon as possible after they are cooked.

蔥薑焗鮮蟹
Braised Crabs with Green Onion

材料：
花蟹或青蟹大的1隻或小的2隻、蔥8支、薑1塊

調味料：
酒1大匙、淡色醬油1大匙、鹽1/4茶匙、胡椒粉1/4茶匙、

做法：
1. 蟹可選用海蟹或青蟹、花蟹，買回沖洗外殼後，再打開蟹蓋，將腮、肺等內部摘理乾淨，每隻蟹視大小剖
2. 切為四塊或六塊。
3. 蔥切段，薑切片。
鍋內燒熱3大匙油，放入薑片和2/3量的蔥段鍋爆香，再放下螃蟹，大火快炒至螃蟹外殼轉紅，淋下調味料並注入清水1杯，蓋上鍋蓋燜熟，約4~5分鐘。
4. 起鍋時再撒下剩餘之蔥段，並淋下1大匙油便可裝盤。

* 花蟹味道較鹹，調味時要減少鹽分。

* Some crab taste salty itself, reduce the salt while season the dish.

Ingredients：
1 big live crab or 2 small crabs, 8 stalks green onion, a piece of ginger

Seasonings：
1T. wine, 1T. light colored soy sauce, 1/4t. salt, 1/4t. pepper

Procedures：
1. Choose any kind of live crab or fresh crab. Remove lungs and intestines. Rinse then cut the body into 4 or 6 pieces. Crush the crab claws.
2. Cut the green onion into sections. Slice the ginger.
3. Heat 3T. oil in wok until very hot. Place ginger and 2/3 of the green onion into the wok and stir-fry until fragrant. Add crabs, stir-fry over high heat until the crabs turn red. Sprinkle seasonings, and 1C. water. Cover and cook until the crab is done, about 4~5 minutes.
4. Add rest of the green onion and 1T. oil. Transfer to a platter and serve.

海鮮類

家常魷魚捲
Stir-fried Squid Rolls with Chili Sauce

材料：
水發魷魚1條、絞肉2兩、薑屑1/2大匙、芹菜段1杯、蔥屑2大匙

調味料：
辣豆瓣醬1大匙、酒1大匙、淡色醬油1大匙、鹽1/4茶匙、糖1/2茶匙、太白粉1茶匙、麻油少許

做法：
1. 將魷魚撕去薄膜後，直切成兩半並在內部切入交叉之細密刀口，然後分割切成3公分寬、4公分長之斜塊，全部用開水燙至捲起、立刻撈出（如果不立刻下鍋炒時，要把魷魚泡在水中）。
2. 起油鍋用2大匙油先炒絞肉、薑屑和辣豆瓣醬，加入芹菜段並淋下酒、醬油及鹽、糖調味。
3. 放下魷魚炒合，並淋下太白粉水炒勻，撒下蔥屑、淋下麻油即好。

Ingredients：
1 soaked dried squid, 75g. ground pork, 1/2T. chopped ginger, 1C. celery sections, 2T. chopped green onion

Seasonings：
1T. hot bean paste, 1T. wine, 1T. light colored soy sauce, 1/4t. salt, 1/2t. sugar, 1t. cornstarch paste, 1/4t. sesame oil

Procedures：
1. Remove one layer of membrane from the outside of the squid. Score the inside lengthwise and crosswise. Then cut into pieces 3cm wide × 4cm long. Blanch for 5 seconds (if the squid is not stir-fried immediately, soak it in cold water).
2. Heat 2T. oil in a wok. Stir-fry the ground pork, ginger, and hot bean paste. Add celery. Sprinkle with wine, then season with soy sauce, salt, and sugar.
3. Place squid in wok, stir-fry for a few seconds. Thicken with cornstarch paste. Stir-fry thoroughly. Sprinkle green onion and sesame oil, mix and serve hot.

宮保蟹腿肉
Crab Legs with Gung-Bao Sauce

材料：

蟹腿肉1盒、小黃瓜1條、油炸花生米1/3杯、
薑屑1茶匙、蒜屑2茶匙、花椒粒1大匙、乾辣椒8支
蛋麵糊：蛋1個、麵粉4大匙、太白粉4大匙、水適量

調味料：

（1）鹽1/4茶匙、酒1茶匙、胡椒粉少許
（2）醬油2大匙、酒1/2大匙、糖1茶匙、水1/3杯、
太白粉1茶匙、麻油1/2茶匙

做法：

1. 蟹腿肉解凍後略加沖洗，輕輕將每一條分開，拌上調味料（1）醃10分鐘。
2. 小黃瓜一切為4直條、去子、切斜段；花生去衣。
3. 蟹腿肉上撒少許乾麵粉，再沾上調好的蛋麵糊，投入熱油中炸熟且脆。小黃瓜也過油炸一下。
4. 用2大匙油炒香花椒粒，撈棄。再將乾辣椒段放入炒至變色，同時放入薑、蒜屑、黃瓜等，淋下調味料（2），拌炒均勻，關火，加入蟹腿肉和花生米便可。

Ingredients：

1 box crab legs, 1 cucumber, 1/3C. fried peanuts,
1t. chopped ginger, 2t. chopped garlic,
1T. brown peppercorn, 8 pieces dried red chili

Flour batter： 1 egg, 4T. flour, 4T. cornstarch, water

Seasonings：

（1）1/4t. salt, 1t. wine, pepper
（2）2T. soy sauce, 1/2T. wine, 1t. sugar, 1/3C. water,
1t. cornstarch, 1/2t. sesame oil

Procedures：

1. Defrost the crab legs, rinse slightly. Separate each one, mix with seasonings (1) for 10 minutes.
2. Cut cucumber into 4 stripes, remove seeds, cut diagonally；peel the peanuts.
3. Sprinkle some flour on crab legs, coat with flour batter. Deep-fry in hot oil until done and crispy. Drain. deep-fry cucumber for 10 seconds, drain.
4. Stir-fry brown peppercorn until fragrant, discard it. Fry diced dried red chili until the color changed, add chopped ginger and garlic, fry for a while, put cucumber and seasonings (2), stir evenly. Turn off the heat, add crab legs and peanuts in. Serve hot.

海鮮類

海鮮類

82

八寶釀鮮魷
Stuffed Squid

材料：
新鮮魷魚2條、蔥花2大匙、香菇2朵、蝦米2大匙、火腿或臘腸丁1/2杯、雞肫1個、糯米飯1杯、蔥1支、薑2片

調味料：
（1）醬油2茶匙、鹽1/2茶匙、胡椒粉1/4茶匙
（2）酒1大匙、醬油2大匙、糖1/3茶匙、胡椒粉1/4茶匙、水2杯、太白粉水1大匙

做法：
1. 將魷魚內臟抽出，沖洗後擦乾，抹上少許太白粉在腹內。
2. 起油鍋炒香蔥花、香菇（泡軟、切小丁）、蝦米（泡軟、摘好）、火腿、雞肫、和切粒的魷魚腳，淋下調味料（1），大火拌炒至有香氣。關火，加入糯米飯拌勻。
3. 將糯米餡分別填塞到魷魚中（不可太滿），並用牙籤封住開口處。
4. 起油鍋煎香蔥、薑，淋下酒與醬油後將魷魚放下，加入糖、胡椒粉及水，用小火燒煮約10分鐘左右。
5. 取出魷魚趁熱切成1 1/2公分寬度，按原形排列碟中。鍋中之湯汁淋下太白粉水少許勾芡，澆到魷魚上即可。

Ingredients：
2 fresh squid, 2 T. chopped green onion, 2 black mushrooms, 3T. dried shrimp (soaked), 1/2C. diced ham, 1 chicken gizzard, 1C. cooked glutinous rice, 1stalk green onion, 2 slices ginger

Seasonings：
（1）2t. soy sauce, 1/2t. salt, 1/4t. pepper
（2）1T. wine, 2T. soy sauce, 1/3t. sugar, 1/4t. pepper, 2C. water, 1T. cornstarch paste

Procedures:
1. Remove the heads and intestines from the fresh squid. Rinse and pat dry. Peel the squid feet and dice. Sprinkle some cornstarch inside of the squid.
2. Heat 2 T. oil to stir-fry green onion, black mushrooms (soaked and diced), dried shrimp (soaked and trim), ham, diced chicken gizzard, and diced squid feet. Season with seasonings (1), stir-fry for about 1 minute. Turn off the heat, add glutinous rice and mix thoroughly.
3. Stuff glutinous rice into the squid (do not stuff too full). Seal each squid with toothpick.
4. Heat 2T. oil to fry ginger and green onion. Sprinkle with wine and soy sauce, then add squid, sugar, pepper, and water. Simmer for 10 minutes.
5. Remove the squid, cut into pieces 1 1/2cm wide. Arrange on a platter. Thicken the liquid with cornstarch paste, pour over squid and serve.

海鮮類

84

三鮮鍋巴

Popped Rice with Seafood Sauce

材料：
海參1條、蝦仁3兩、瘦豬肉2兩、豌豆莢12片、熟筍1支、鍋巴8片、蔥2支、薑2片

調味料：
（1）鹽1/4茶匙、太白粉1茶匙
（2）酒1大匙、清湯2杯、醬油1大匙、鹽1/2茶匙、太白粉水1大匙

做法：

1. 海參洗淨、除去肚內之腸子後，放在一小鍋中，加清水2杯及少許蔥、薑、酒，以小火煮20分鐘。取出直切為二、再斜刀切成大薄片；瘦肉煮熟後亦切成片。
2. 蝦仁用鹽抓洗、沖淨、擦乾後，用調味料（1）醃上10分鐘；豌豆莢摘好，用開水燙半分鐘，沖冷水；筍切片。
3. 1杯油燒至八分熱，將蝦仁放入、過油炒熟，撈出瀝乾。
4. 另將3大匙油燒熱後，放入蔥、薑爆香，淋1大匙酒、隨即注入清湯，並加醬油、鹽調味。加入海參、肉片、筍片、豌豆莢，用大火煮滾，淋下太白粉水勾芡，再將蝦仁落鍋拌勻，改用小火保溫。
5. 鍋中將炸油燒得極熱後，投下鍋巴，用大火將鍋巴炸得膨脹（用鏟子翻拌），至顏色金黃而酥脆時，立即撈出、裝在深盤中。
6. 待鍋巴炸好後，將三鮮料用碗盛著，與鍋巴一同上桌，並馬上將三鮮料澆在鍋巴上，趁發出油爆聲時迅予分食。

Ingredients：
1 sea cucumber (or black mushrooms), 100g. shrimp, 80g. lean pork, 12 snow pea pots, 1 cooked bamboo shoot, 8 pieces popped rice, 2 stalks green onion, 2 slices ginger

Seasonings：
（1）1/4t. salt, 1t. cornstarch
（2）1T. wine, 2C. soup stock, 1T. soy sauce, 1/2t. salt, 1T. cornstarch paste

Procedures：

1. Clean the soaked sea cucumber. Cook in 2C. water with 1 stalk green onion, 2 slices ginger, and 1T. wine for 20 minutes. Cut in half lengthwise and slice into thin pieces (if black mushrooms are used, soak in water until soft). Cook the lean pork, then slice it.
2. Rinse the shrimp and marinate with seasonings (1) for 10 minutes ; boil the snow pea pots, then soak in cold water ; slice the cooked bamboo shoot.
3. Heat 1C. oil to 160°C. Fry the shrimp for 10 seconds. Drain.
4. Heat only 3T. oil to fry green onion and ginger. Sprinkle with wine, add 2C. soup stock immediately, season with soy sauce and salt. Add sea cucumber, pork, bamboo shoots, and snow pea pots. Bring to a boil, thicken with cornstarch paste. Add shrimp. This is the sauce.
5. Heat 4C. oil until very hot. Deep-fry popped rice (stir with spatula). When it becomes golden brown and crispy, drain and place on a large platter.
6. Serve the popped rice and the sauce (serve in a bowl) together. Pour sauce on top of popped rice at the table.

海鮮類

86

酸辣海參
Sea Cucumber with Minced Pork

材料：

海參4條（約12兩重）、絞肉2兩、熟筍1支、薑末1茶匙、蔥粒1大匙、芹菜屑1大匙

煮海參料： 蔥、薑各少許、酒1/2大匙、清水4杯

調味料：

酒1/2大匙、醬油2大匙、清湯2杯、糖1/4茶匙、鹽1/2茶匙、太白粉水1大匙、醋1大匙、胡椒粉1/4茶匙

做法：

1. 買已發好了的海參時，應選擇軟度相同的。每條肚內的腸筋要清除乾淨，放在鍋內，加入煮海參料，用小火煮約10分鐘，以除去海參腥味。
2. 煮好的海參用冷水沖洗之後，切成5公分長的直絲（如海參太厚須先片開）；煮熟之筍子亦切細絲。
3. 鍋中燒熱3大匙油，爆炒薑末及絞肉，並淋下酒及醬油，注入清湯煮滾。放進海參絲及筍絲，加糖、鹽再煮滾一次，用太白粉水勾芡，淋下醋及胡椒粉，撒下蔥粒及芹菜屑，速加拌合即熄火裝盤。

Ingredients：

4 pieces sea cucumber (about 450g.), 80g. ground pork, 1 cooked bamboo shoot, 1t. chopped ginger, 1T. chopped green onion, 1T. chopped celery

To cook sea cucumber： 1stalk green onion, 2 slices ginger, 1/2T. wine, 4C. water

Seasonings：

1/2T. wine, 2T. soy sauce, 2C. soup stock, 1/4t. sugar, 1/2t.salt, 1T. cornstarch paste, 1T. vinegar, 1/4t. pepper

Procedures：

1. Clean sea cucumber. Cook with green onion, ginger, wine, and water over low heat for 10 minutes to remove the fishy flavor from the sea cucumber.
2. Rinse the cooked sea cucumber with cold water. Shred it into strings 5cm long (if the sea cucumber is too thick, slice it in half horizontally, then shred)；shred the cooked bamboo shoot.
3. Heat 3T. oil in wok. Stir-fry the ground pork and ginger. Sprinkle with wine and soy sauce, add soup stock. Bring to a boil. Add sea cucumber and bamboo shoots. Season with sugar and salt. After boiling, thicken with cornstarch paste. Add vinegar, pepper, chopped green onions, and celery. Mix well and remove to a large soup bowl. Serve.

* 乾海參之發法：海參用清水泡6小時後刷乾淨，再放入砂鍋中，加清水以小火煮半小時，熄火後燜至水冷。取出海參剪開腹部，清除腸子，再換清水泡過、並煮半小時，燜至冷水，如此重複三、四次，至海參已夠軟大了便可。

* **To soak the dried sea cucumber：** Soak with cold water for 6 hours, clean and place in a large pot. Add enough water to cover the sea cucumber, cook for 1/2 hour. Turn off the heat, soak until the water cools. The pot must be covered.

* Cut open the bottom side of the sea cucumber and clean. Soak with clean water, then simmer for 1/2 hour again and let stand until it cools. Repeat 3 or 4 times, until the sea cucumber is soft.

墨魚大燴
Stewed Cuttlefish with Pork

材料：
五花肉12兩、墨魚12兩、薑3片、蔥2支、八角1顆

調味料：
酒2大匙、醬油4大匙、紅豆腐乳汁1大匙、冰糖1大匙、水2 1/2杯

做法：
1. 五花肉切成3公分寬之塊狀；墨魚切成3×5公分之長方形。
2. 鍋內放下2大匙油爆香薑片、蔥段和八角，再放下肉塊，以大火將肉塊煎黃。待已透出香氣後，淋下酒並加醬油及紅豆腐乳汁、糖、水，蓋緊鍋蓋，以大火煮滾後再以小火燜約半小時。
3. 將墨魚塊加入，繼續燜煮半小時，至湯汁約剩半杯左右，開大火燴煮以收乾湯汁，使其濃稠。可撒下青蒜絲或香菜上桌。

*如果沒有紅豆腐乳汁，亦可不用，則醬油的份量要增加1大匙。

***If you do not use the salted red bean curd juice, use an additional 1T. soy sauce.**

Ingredients：
450g. pork, 450g. cuttlefish, 3 slices ginger, 2 stalks green onion, 1 star anise

Seasonings：
2T. wine, 4T. soy sauce,
1T. salted red bean curd juice (optional), 1T. rock sugar,
2 1/2 C. water

Procedures：
1. Cut the pork into 3cm cubes；cut cuttlefish into pieces 3cm×5cm.
2. Stir-fry ginger, green onion (cut 2" long) and star anise with 2T. oil. Add pork. Fry until the pork becomes brown. Add wine, soy sauce, salted red bean curd juice, rock sugar, and water. Bring to a boil, then simmer for 1/2 hour.
3. Add cuttlefish, simmer for another 1/2 hour until 1/2 C. of sauce remains. Turn to high heat to reduce the sauce. Remove to a platter. You may garnish with parsley or green garlic.

蔥燒鯽魚
Braised Fish with Green Onion

材料：
小鯽魚1斤、蔥1/2斤、麻油1/2茶匙

調味料：
(1) 醬油3大匙、酒1大匙、醋2大匙
(2) 醬油3大匙、醋2大匙、酒1大匙、糖1大匙、水3杯

做法：
1. 選購約12~13公分長之小鯽魚，清理乾淨後，用調味料（1）醃泡半小時左右，（在醃時需時常加以翻動，以使魚能均勻的吸收調味料）。
2. 鍋燒熱後放入1杯油，將魚下鍋煎黃兩面。
3. 將半斤蔥洗淨、一切為兩段，用油3大匙煎到黃而有香氣。將魚放在蔥上，淋下調味料（2），蓋上鍋蓋、用小火燒煮1小時半至2個小時。見湯汁收乾為止，淋下麻油，搖動幾下鍋子便可盛出，待涼後風味更佳。

Ingredients：
600g. small gold carp, 300g. green onion, 1/2t. sesame oil

Seasonings：
(1) 3T. soy sauce, 1T. wine, 2T. vinegar
(2) 3T. soy sauce, 2T. vinegar, 1T. wine, 1T. sugar, 3C. water

Procedures：
1. Choose small fish — about 12~13cm long. Rinse and pat dry. Marinate with seasonings (1) for 1 hour. Turn them over often while soaking, so the marinade will be absorbed evenly.
2. Heat 1C. oil in wok. Fry the fish over high until both sides get golden brown. Remove.
3. Trim the green onions and cut into halves. Fry the green onion with 3T. oil until brown and fragrant. Place the fish on top of the green onions. Add seasonings (2). Cover and simmer for 1 1/2~2 hours. When all the liquid is absorbed, sprinkle sesame oil and serve while it get cool.

辣豆瓣魚
Carp with Hot Bean Sauce

材料：
活鯉魚1條或其他活魚亦可、豆腐1塊、薑屑1大匙、大蒜屑1大匙、酒釀1大匙

調味料：
（1）辣豆瓣醬2大匙、酒1大匙、醬油2大匙、鹽1/2茶匙、糖2茶匙、水2杯
（2）太白粉水少許、鎮江醋1/2大匙、麻油1茶匙、蔥花1大匙

做法：
1. 鯉魚打理乾淨後，擦乾水分，在魚身上斜切2~3條刀紋。
2. 鍋中燒熱油5大匙，將魚的兩面稍微煎一下，盛出。放入薑、蒜末爆香，再放入辣豆瓣醬和酒釀同炒，淋下調味料（1）一起煮滾，放回魚和豆腐，一起燒煮約10分鐘。
3. 見汁已剩一半時，將魚和豆腐盛出裝盤。湯汁勾芡，並加調味料（2）炒勻，把汁淋在魚身上。

Ingredients:
1 carp or other live fish, 1piece bean curd, 1T. chopped ginger, 1T. chopped garlic, 1T. sweet fermented rice

Seasonings:
（1）2T. hot bean paste, 1T. wine, 2T. soy sauce, 1/2t. salt, 2t. sugar, 2C. water
（2）a little of cornstarch paste, 1/2T. brown vinegar, 1t. sesame oil, 1T. green onion

Procedures:
1. Rinse and pat dry the carp. Score 2~3 times on both sides.
2. Heat 5T. oil in wok, fry the fish lightly, remove. Add ginger and garlic, fry until fragrant, add hot bean paste, fermented rice, and all seasonings (1), bring to a boil, return carp and bean curd in, stew for 10 minutes.
3. When juice reduce to half, remove carp and bean curd to a plate. Thicken the juice, add (2), mix evenly, pour over carp.

乾燒帶魚
Braised Fish with Brown Sauce

材料：
新鮮帶魚1條（約12兩重）、蔥段（1寸長）15段、大蒜片5片、麵粉2大匙

調味料：
（1）鹽1/3茶匙、酒1大匙、醬油2大匙
（2）醋1/2大匙、糖1茶匙、水1杯

做法：
1. 將帶魚身上銀色之魚鱗刮掉，並切下背鰭，沖洗一下、瀝乾水分，在兩面先切入0.5公分間隔之刀口，再分切成5公分寬小段。
2. 全部用調味料（1）拌過，醃15分鐘，再沾上麵粉。
3. 鍋子先燒熱，放下3大匙油再燒熱，迅速放下帶魚段，用大火煎至魚肉酥黃（每面約需2分鐘）。
4. 放下大蒜片及蔥段煎香，淋下剩餘之酒及醬油，再放下醋、糖及清水，蓋鍋燒約10分鐘，再以大火收乾汁液，便可裝碟。

Ingredients：
1 hair tail (about 450g.), 15pieces green onion section, 5 slices garlic, 2T. flour

Seasonings：
（1） 1/3t.sal, 1T. wine, 2T. soy sauce
（2） 1/2T. vinegar, 1t. sugar, 1C. water

Procedures：
1. Trim the fish, cut off the back fins. Rinse and pat it dry. Score the fish and cut into pieces 5cm long.
2. Soak the fish with seasonings (1) for 15 minutes. Coat with flour.
3. Heat 3T. oil in the wok. fry both sides of the fish over high heat until brown (about 2 minutes for each side).
4. Add garlic slices and green onion. Fry until fragrant. Sprinkle the remaining soy sauce and seasonings (2). Cook over low heat for 10 minutes. Remove to a plate when the sauce is reduced.

＊ 如欲將魚煎得酥脆又不破時，油不可用得太多，開始時火力要強，封住表面，再改小火慢煎。
＊ **If you want the fish to be crispy and keep the shape after frying, don't use too much oil. Fry over high heat at the beginning, and when the surface become hard, turn to low heat and continue to fry.**

魚類

豆酥鯧魚
Steamed Fish with Yellow Bean Sauce

材料：
鯧魚1條（約12兩）、黃豆豉1/2球、大蒜屑1/2大匙、薑末1茶匙、蔥末 2大匙

調味料：
（1）鹽1/2茶匙、酒1大匙、胡椒粉少許
（2）辣豆瓣醬1/2茶匙、酒1茶匙、糖1/4茶匙、麻油少許

做法：

1. 將鯧魚洗淨，兩面各切兩道斜刀口，撒上調味料（1）醃一下。放入盤中（盤下可鋪細蔥5~6支）。上鍋用大火蒸熟（約12分鐘），取出後換到另一只乾淨的大盤中。
2. 黃豆豉切碎，用3大匙油將豆豉炒香，並放下薑末和蒜末再炒至十分鬆乾，淋下調味料（2），撒下蔥花，再淋下熱油1大匙，大火拌炒至酥香起泡時，全部澆到鯧魚身上便可。

Ingredients：
1 pomfret (about 450g.), 1/2 fermented yellow beans, 1/2T. chopped garlic, 1t. chopped ginger, 2T. chopped green onion

Seasonings：
（1）1/2t. salt, 1T. wine, a pinch of pepper
（2）1/2t. hot bean paste, 1t. wine, 1/4t. sugar, sesame oil

Procedures:

1. Trim the fish, cut 2 diagonal slashes on each side. Marinate with seasonings (1). Place on a platter (arrange 5 or 6 green onions on the platter first). Steam for 15 minutes. Transfer to a clean platter.
2. Chop the fermented yellow beans , and stir-fry with 3T. oil. Add ginger, and garlic in, stir-fry until very dry. Add seasonings (2), and 1T. hot oil. Stir-fry over high heat until the mixture bubbles. Add green onions, pour the sauce over the top of the fish. Serve.

* 除鯧魚外黃魚、鯢魚或石斑魚、鱈魚或魚片均可使用。明蝦或草蝦也可用此方法烹調。

* **In addition to pomfret, you may use grouper or yellow fish or cod or fish fillet . This technique may also be used to cook prawns.**

魚類

魚類

西湖醋魚
West Lake Fish

材料：
活草魚中段一段（約1斤重）、蔥2支、薑2片、嫩薑絲1/2杯、清水3杯、
白胡椒粉少許

調味料：
酒1大匙、醬油2大匙、糖3大匙、鹽1/2茶匙、鎮江醋4大匙、醬色2茶匙（可不用）、
藕粉（或太白粉）水1大匙、麻油1/4茶匙

做法：
1. 將活魚剖殺，洗淨後，取用中間一段，再橫片成兩片，魚肉太厚處、也可切直刀刀口。
2. 在鍋內燒滾開水（加蔥支、薑片同燒），將魚皮朝上、放入滾水中燙煮，待水再沸滾後，改用小火煮約2~3分鐘，在魚肉最厚處以一支筷子插試，熟了便速予熄火、撈出裝在盤內。
3. 嫩薑絲用冰開水泡一下後，擠乾放在盤中魚之身上。
4. 將油2大匙燒熱，淋下酒爆香，隨即加入清湯2杯（可用燙魚之水），並放調味料煮滾，最後澆下另1大匙熱油及麻油，便可全部淋在盤內魚上面（撒下少許胡椒），趁熱上桌即可。

Ingredients：
600g. fresh water fish, 2 stalks green onion, 2 slices ginger, 1/2C. shredded ginger,
3C. water, a pinch of pepper

Seasonings：
1T. wine, 2T. dark colored soy sauce, 3T. sugar, 1/2t. salt, 4T. vinegar,
2t. brown food color (optional), 1T. cornstarch paste, 1/4t. sesame oil

Procedures:
1. Trim and scale the fish. Halve it, if the meat part is too thick, make 1~2 cuts.
2. Boil green onion and ginger with 4C. water. Place the fish in the water. Bring to a boil, then simmer for 2~3 minutes until done (you may use a chopstick to test whether the fish is done). Drain and place on a serving platter.
3. Soak the shredded ginger in iced water for 1 minute. Squeeze and place on top of fish.
4. Heat 2T. oil in wok, add wine and 2C. soup stock (remaining from cooking the fish). Add seasonings. After boiling, thicken with cornstarch paste. Add 1T. hot oil. Pour the sauce on top of fish (you may sprinkle a little pepper on the fish). Serve hot.

魚類

大蒜黃魚
Stewed Yellow Croaker with Garlic

材料：
大黃魚或其他新鮮魚1條（約450公克重）、香菇3朵、粉皮2張、大蒜粒10粒、蔥5小段、青蒜半支

調味料：
(1) 鹽1/2茶匙、醬油2大匙
(2) 酒1大匙、醬油3大匙、糖1大匙、水3杯、胡椒粉少許

做法：
1. 黃魚兩面各切兩、三條斜刀痕（也可以切成2段），用調味料（1）抹勻、放置5~10分鐘。香菇泡軟切片。
2. 用熱油把黃魚兩面煎黃，盛出魚。放入大蒜爆香，再放入蔥段和香菇炒香，加入調味料（2）和魚，先以大火煮滾，再改小火，蓋好鍋蓋，燒約20分鐘至湯汁剩下1杯左右。
3. 加入切寬條的粉皮，煮至粉皮透明，撒下切好之青蒜絲即可裝盤。

Ingredients:
1 fresh fish (about 450g.), 3 black mushrooms, 2 pieces mung bean sheet, 10 cloves garlic, 5 green onion sections, 1/2 green garlic

Seasonings:
(1) 1/2t. salt, 2T. soy sauce
(2) 1T. wine, 3T. soy sauce, 1T. sugar, 3C. water, pepper

Procedures：
1. Score 2~3 times on both sides of fish or cut the fish into two sections, rub with seasonings (1). Soak and slice black mushrooms.
2. Heat 5T. oil to fry both sides of the fish, Remove. Add garlic, fry until brown and fragrant, add green onion and black mushroom, stir-fry together until fragrant. Add seasonings (2) and fish, bring to a boil over high heat, reduce to low, simmer for 20 minutes until the liquid reduce to 1 cup.
3. Add mung bean sheet sections, cook until it becomes soft, sprinkle shredded green garlic on top, remove to the serving plate.

雙味魚捲
Two Flavored Fish Rolls

材料：
白色魚肉300公克、熟筍絲1/2杯、豆腐衣4張

調味料：
(1) 鹽1/2茶匙、蛋白1大匙、油1大匙、麻油1茶匙、胡椒粉1/6茶匙、蔥屑1大匙、薑汁1/2茶匙

(2) 蒜屑1/2大匙、蔥花1大匙、番茄醬2大匙、糖2大匙、醋2大匙、水4大匙、鹽1/4茶匙、太白粉少許、麻油少許

做法：
1. 魚肉切成小丁。大碗中將調味料（1）調勻，再放入魚肉拌勻，醃約10分鐘，拌入筍絲。
2. 豆腐衣每張切成3小張，包入適量的魚肉，包捲成小春捲形。
3. 用1大匙油爆香蒜屑和蔥花，再加入其他調勻的調味料（2）煮滾，盛裝小碟中。
4. 鍋中炸油燒至八分熱，放入魚捲小火炸約1分鐘，改大火炸成金黃色，撈出，瀝乾油分，裝盤。附上五香花椒鹽和甜酸汁上桌。

＊五香花椒鹽：參考53頁花椒鹽的做法，再加少許五香粉拌勻即可。

Ingredients:
300g. fish fillet, 1/2C. shredded bamboo shoot (cooked), 4 pieces dried soy bean sheet

Seasonings:
1/2t. salt, 1T. egg white, 1T. oil, 1t. sesame oil, 1/6t. pepper, 1T. chopped green onion, 1/2t. ginger juice

1/2T. chopped garlic, 1T. chopped green onion, 2T. ketchup, 2T. sugar, 2T. vinegar, 4T. water, 1/4t. salt, cornstarch, sesame oil

Procedures:
1. Cut fish into small pieces. Marinate with mixed seasonings (1) for 10 minutes. Add bamboo shoot and leek.
2. Divide each bean curd sheet into 3 small pieces, wrap fish mixture into small pack.
3. Stir-fry garlic and green onion with 1T. oil, add other seasonings (2) to make the sweet & sour sauce.
4. Deep-fry fish rolls with 160°C oil for about 1 minute over low heat, turn to high heat at last 20 seconds. Drain, serve with brown pepper salt and sweet & sour sauce.

＊**The recipe for brown peppercorn salt is on page 53. You may add spicy powder in it.**

蠔油魚片
Fish Fillet with Oyster Sauce

材料：
白色魚肉6兩（240公克）、熟筍片、熟胡蘿蔔片、豌豆片、草菇各適量、蔥2支、薑片8小片

調味料
(1) 鹽1/4茶匙、酒1/2大匙、蛋白1大匙、太白粉1/2大匙
(2) 蠔油2大匙、糖1/4茶匙、水4大匙、太白粉1/2茶匙、麻油少許

做法：
1. 魚肉片切成約0.5公分的厚片，用調味料（1）拌勻醃30分鐘左右。
2. 草菇和豌豆片分別用滾水川燙一下，泡冷水備用。
3. 1杯油先熱至八分熱，放下魚片過油至熟，撈出。
4. 用2大匙油爆香蔥段和薑片，放下配料炒數下，再將魚片放入鍋中，淋下調味料（2），輕輕拌炒均勻便可。

Ingredients:
240g. fish fillet (white meat), cooked bamboo shoot slices, cooked carrot slices, snow pea pots, straw mushrooms, 2 stalks green onion, 8 slices ginger

Seasonings:
(1) 1/4t. salt, 1/2T. wine, 1T. egg white, 1/2T. cornstarch
(2) 2T. oyster sauce, 1/4t. sugar, 4T. water, 1/2t. cornstarch, a few drops of sesame oil

Procedures:
1. Slice fish into 0.5cm thick slices, marinate with seasonings (1) for 30 minutes.
2. Blanch straw mushrooms and snow pa pots, drain and rinse with cold water.
3. Heat 1C. oil to 160°C, fry fish until just done, drain.
4. Heat 2T. oil to stir-fry green onion (cut into 3cm long) and ginger first, add vegetables and fish, pour mixed seasonings (2), stir-fry carefully and quickly until evenly mixed. Remove to the serving plate.

酥炸魚條
Deep-fried Crispy Fish

材料：
新鮮魚肉250公克、麵粉2大匙

醃魚料： 蛋白1大匙、鹽1/2茶匙、太白粉1茶匙、酒2茶匙、蔥1支（拍碎）、薑汁1/2茶匙

麵糊料： 蛋1個、太白粉3大匙、麵粉2大匙、鹽1/4茶匙、發泡粉1/2大匙、冰水酌量、油1大匙

做法：

1. 魚肉切成如小拇指般粗細的長條。醃魚料先調勻，再將魚條放入拌合，醃20分鐘以上。
2. 蛋打散，依序加入麵糊料調勻成糊狀，最後落油拌勻。
3. 魚條先撒上少許乾麵粉後拌入麵糊中。
4. 3杯油燒至八分熱時改成小火，盡量分散魚條，一一投入油中。再開中火來炸。見魚條全部浮起，用筷子將黏在一起的魚條分開，再以大火炸20秒鐘，使外表酥脆便可撈出裝盤。附沾料上桌。

＊ 沾料可選用花椒鹽、番茄醬、沙拉醬、糖醋汁或蘿蔔泥柴魚汁。

Ingredients:
250g. fish fillet, 2T. flour

Seasonings:
1T. egg white, 1/2t. salt, 1t. cornstarch, 2t. wine, 1 stalk crushed green onion

Flour paste: 1 egg, 3T. cornstarch, 2T. flour, 1/4t. salt, 1/2T. baking powder, some ice water, 1T. oil

Procedures:

1. Cut fish into strips (size about the little finger). Marinate with the mixed seasonings for 20 minutes.
2. Beat egg, add cornstarch, flour, salt and some water to make paste. Add oil at last.
3. Mix fish with 2T. flour, add into flour paste.
4. Heat 3 cups of oil to 160°C, deep-fry fish separately over low heat. Turn to medium heat, deep-fry until all flow up. Deep-fry over high heat for the last 20 secords, drain. Serve with dipping sauce.

＊ **You may choose brown peppercorn salt, or ketchup, or mayonnaise, or sweet & sour sauce, or Japanese style sauce as the dipping sauce.**

魚類

廣式清蒸魚
Steamed Fish, Cantonese Style

材料：

新鮮魚1條（約450公克）、蔥3支、薑絲3湯匙、蔥絲半杯、香菜段半杯

調味料：

醬油3大匙、糖1/2茶匙、水3大匙、白胡椒粉少許

做法：

1. 魚打理乾淨，擦乾水分。魚身的兩面均劃上刀口；蔥切成長段。
2. 盤子上墊上蔥段，放上魚後、撒上薑絲，移入蒸籠內大火蒸約10~11分鐘，至魚熟後端出。倒出蒸魚汁，夾掉蔥段，撒下白胡椒粉。
3. 炒鍋中燒熱2大匙油，淋下調勻的調味料，一滾即關火，撒下蔥絲，全部淋在魚身上，同時來回多澆淋數次以使魚入味。

Ingredients:

1 fresh fish (about 450g.), 3 stalks green onion, 2T. shredded ginger, 1/2C. shredded green onion, 1/2C. cilantro sections

Seasonings:

3T. soy sauce, 1/2t. sugar, 3T. water, a pinch of white pepper

Procedure:

1. Rinse fish, pat dry. Scored 2 or 3 times on each side. Cut green onion into long sections, place on the steaming plate.
2. Put fish on, sprinkle ginger over fish, steam with high heat for about 10~11 minutes, try with a chopstick to make sure that the fish is done. Pour away the liquid from steaming fish, discard green onion, sprinkle pepper on.
3. Heat 2T. oil, pour mixed seasonings in, turn off the heat when it boils, put green onion shreds in sauce, pour over fish.

糖醋溜全魚
Sweet & Sour Fish

材料：

長型魚1條（約1斤重）、洋蔥丁1/2杯、番茄丁1/2杯、香菇丁2湯匙、青豆2湯匙、太白粉1/2杯

調味料：

(1) 蔥1支、薑2片、鹽2/3茶匙、酒1大匙
(2) 番茄醬3大匙、糖4大匙、醋4大匙、鹽1/4茶匙、水1/2杯、太白粉1/2大匙、麻油1茶匙

做法：

1. 魚打理乾淨，在兩面魚身上，用刀切深而薄、並可翹起的的刀紋，用調味料（1）醃20分鐘。
2. 用太白粉沾裹魚身各處，仔細沾緊。投入熱油中炸兩次至酥而脆，撈出，瀝乾油。站放在大盤中。
3. 用2大匙油先炒香洋蔥，再放入香菇和番茄丁，並將調勻的調味料（2）倒入煮滾，全部淋在魚身上。

＊可以用黃魚、鯨魚、草魚、鱸魚來做這道菜。只要是長型並且夠新鮮即可。

＊There are many kinds of fish you may use, as long as it is a long shaped fish and is fresh enough.

Ingredients:

1 long shaped fish (about 600g.), 1/2C. diced onion, 1/2C. diced tomato, 2T. diced black mushroom, 2T. snow peas, 1/2C. cornstarch

Seasonings:

(1) 1 stalk green onion, 2 slices ginger, 2/3t. salt, 1T. wine
(2) 3T. ketchup, 4T. sugar, 4T. vinegar, 1/4t. salt, 1/2C. water, 1/2T. cornstarch, 1t. sesame oil

Procedures:

1. Rinse fish, score diagonally on both sides of fish. Marinate with seasonings (1) for 20 minutes.
2. Coat fish tightly with cornstarch, deep-fry in hot oil twice to get the crispy outside. Place on serving plate.
3. Stir-fry onion, mushroom and tomato in 2T. oil, add seasonings (2), bring to a boil, add snow peas, pour over fish.

乾燒大魚頭
Stewed Fish Head

材料：

鰱魚頭1個、絞肉2大匙、蔥屑3大匙、薑末1/2大匙、大蒜末1大匙、青蒜絲適量、麻油少許

調味料：

辣豆瓣醬1/2大匙、甜麵醬1/2大匙、酒1大匙、醬油3大匙、糖1/2大匙、甜酒釀1/2大匙、胡椒粉1/4茶匙、水2 1/2杯

做法：

1. 魚頭洗淨擦乾水分，浸在3大匙醬油中泡20分鐘，用熱油煎黃兩面，盛出。
2. 另用3大匙油炒香絞肉、薑末、蒜末和蔥末，加入辣豆瓣醬和甜麵醬炒透，再加其他調味料，大火煮滾後放下魚頭，用小火燉煮。
3. 約20分鐘後翻面再燉燒，燒時並用鏟子將汁往魚頭上淋，至湯汁將收乾時，淋下麻油，撒下青蒜絲即可起鍋。

Ingredients:

1 carp head, 2T. grounded pork, 3T. chopped green onion, 1/2T. chopped ginger, 1T. chopped garlic, green garlic shreds, a few drops of sesame oil

Seasonings:

1/2T. hot bean paste, 1/2T. soy bean paste, 1T. wine, 3T. soy sauce, 1/2T. sugar, 1/2T. fermented sweet rice, 1/4t. pepper, 2 1/2C. water

Procedures:

1. Rinse fish head, marinate with 3T. soy sauce for 20 minutes. Fry with heated oil until both sides becomes brown.
2. Heat another 3T. oil to stir-fry pork, ginger, garlic and green onion, add hot bean paste and soy bean paste, stir-fry until fragrant, add other seasonings, place fish head in after the sauce is boiled, simmer for 20 minutes.
3. Turn the head over, continue to cook, pour sauce over the head while cooking. When sauce is almost absorbed, drop sesame oil and sprinkle green garlic shreds. Remove and serve.

琵琶豆腐
Pipa Shaped Bean Curd Balls

材料：

老豆腐（6公分四方大）4塊、火腿屑2大匙、
荸薺屑2大匙、蔥屑2大匙匙、蔥粒2大匙
拌豆腐料：蛋1個、鹽½茶匙、太白粉1大匙

調味料：

清湯½杯、醬油½大匙、鹽¼茶匙、太白粉2茶匙

做法：

1. 將豆腐用刀面壓碎成泥狀，盛大碗內，加入火腿屑、蔥屑、荸薺屑及拌豆腐料，仔細攪拌均勻。
2. 手上抹少許油，將1大匙豆腐料在手上做成橄欖型丸子，放在塗油的盤子上，做好後一一的投入已燒熱的油中，大火炸黃，撈出裝碟。
3. 用2大匙油炒一下蔥粒，加入清湯、醬油和鹽，煮滾後淋下調水之太白粉勾芡，澆到盤中豆腐上便好。

Ingredients：

4 pieces bean curd (6cm×6cm), 2T. chopped ham,
2T. chopped water chestnuts, 2T. chopped green onion,
2T. diced green onion

Seasonings：

(1) 1 egg, 1/2t. salt, 1T. cornstarch
(2) 1/2C. soup stock, 1/2T. soy sauce, 1/4t. salt, 2t. cornstarch

Procedures：

1. Mash the bean curd and place in a bowl. Add seasonings (1). Mix thoroughly.
2. Put some oil on your hands. Use 1T. of bean curd mixture to make a bean curd ball-olive shaped. Place on an greased dish, make all the bean curd balls. Heat the oil to very hot. Push all the bean curd balls into the oil, deep-fry over high heat until golden brown. Drain, and remove to a platter.
3. Stir-fry green onion with 2T. oil. Add soup stock, soy sauce, and salt. Bring to a boil, thicken with cornstarch paste. Pour over the bean curd balls and serve.

麻婆豆腐
Ma Po's Bean Curd

材料：
嫩豆腐（6公分四方）4塊、絞豬肉（或牛肉）2兩、大蒜屑1茶匙、蔥屑1大匙

調味料：
辣豆瓣醬1大匙、辣椒粉1/3茶匙、淡色醬油2大匙、鹽1/2茶匙、糖1/2茶匙、清湯1杯、太白粉2茶匙、麻油1/2茶匙、花椒粉1茶匙

做法：
1. 將豆腐切除硬邊，再切小丁（約1.5公分四方），全部用滾水川燙一下，撈出後瀝乾。
2. 放3大匙油在炒鍋內，先爆炒豬肉，並加入蒜屑及辣豆瓣醬、辣椒粉炒香，繼續放下醬油、鹽、糖等調味料，再將豆腐落鍋輕輕同拌，注入清湯，燜煮3分鐘左右。
3. 用太白粉水勾芡，輕輕拌鏟均勻，撒下蔥屑，再淋下麻油，裝入盤內，然後將花椒粉撒在豆腐上便成。

 ＊豆腐食時既麻、又辣且鹹而燙，才算標準道地。
 ＊豆腐要等下鍋之前，才切塊，以免切好後水分流失，豆腐就會變老，不滑嫩。

Ingredients：
4 pieces tender bean curd (6cm × 6cm), 80g. ground pork (or beef), 1t. chopped garlic, 1T. chopped green onion

Seasonings：
1T. hot red bean paste, 1/3t. red chili powder, 2T. light colored soy sauce, 1/4t. salt, 1/4t. sugar, 1C. soup stock, 2t. cornstarch, 1/2t. sesame oil, 1t. brown peppercorn powder

Procedures：
1. Remove the hard edge from the bean curd, cut into 1.5cm cubes. Boil for 10 seconds. Drain.
2. Stir-fry ground pork with 3T. oil. Add garlic, hot bean paste, red chili powder in, stir-fry continually. Season with soy sauce, salt and sugar. Add the bean curd and soup stock to the wok, cook for 3 minutes.
3. Thicken bean curd with cornstarch paste, sprinkle with green onion and sesame oil. Remove to a plate. Sprinkle brown peppercorn powder on top , and serve hot.

 ＊ **This dish must serve while it is very spicy and hot.**
 ＊ **Cut the bean curd just before cook it, to keep it from loosing the water, and become hard.**

紅燒豆腐
Braised Bean Curd with Ham

材料：
嫩豆腐（6公分四方）3塊、火腿片6片、胡蘿蔔片10片、筍片10片、香菇（或木耳）3朵、蔥2支

調味料：
醬油2大匙、糖1茶匙、清湯1杯、太白粉水1大匙

做法：
1. 豆腐切成3公分長、1公分厚之長方塊，全部用開水燙煮1分鐘。
2. 香菇泡軟切斜片；蔥切3公分長小段。
3. 鍋中燒熱3大匙油，將蔥段爆香，並放下香菇片、筍片、胡蘿蔔片及火腿片略炒，再加入醬油、糖及清湯，煮滾後，放下豆腐輕輕拌合，改小火慢慢燒，燒約10分鐘至豆腐夠入味。
4. 淋下太白粉水勾芡（一面搖動鍋子，一面淋到湯內），待湯汁變濃稠時，由鍋邊再淋下1大匙油，即可全部鏟到盤內。

＊豆腐也可切厚片、油炸一下再燒。

＊**You may also deep-fry or fry the bean curd before cook it, instead of boiled it.**

Ingredients:
3 pieces bean curd (6cm×6cm), 6 slices ham, 10 slices carrot, 10 slices bamboo shoot, 3 black mushrooms, 2 stalks green onion

Seasonings:
2T. soy sauce, 1t. sugar, 1C. soup stock, 1T. cornstarch paste

Procedures:
1. Cut the bean curd into pieces (3cm long×1cm thick). Boil in water for 1 minute.
2. Soak the black mushrooms and slice it. Cut the green onions into pieces 3cm long.
3. Heat 3T. oil to stir-fry green onion. Add black mushrooms, bamboo shoots, carrots, and ham. Stir-fry for 10 seconds. Add soy sauce, sugar, and soup stock. Bring to a boil. Add bean curd in, simmer for 10 minutes.
4. Thicken with cornstarch paste (pour the cornstarch paste in while shaking the wok—do not stir). Add 1T. oil, then transfer to a serving plate.

炒豆腐乾絲
Stir-fried Bean Curd Strings

材料：
白豆腐乾6兩（或白色大豆腐乾4塊）、瘦豬肉2兩、毛豆2大匙、蔥3支

調味料：
（1）醬油1茶匙、太白粉1茶匙、水1/2大匙
（2）醬油1大匙、糖1/2茶匙、鹽1/3茶匙、水3大匙

做法：
1. 選用白豆腐乾，先橫片成半公分之薄片，再切成如二支火柴棒合併的粗細，用熱水燙一下。
2. 瘦肉亦切成細絲，用調味料（1）拌醃5分鐘；蔥切成1.5公分長之小段。
3. 毛豆用水煮2分鐘，撈出沖冷水備用。
4. 將肉絲先用4大匙油炒熟後盛出，再用鍋中剩下的油將蔥段爆香，至蔥段微黃時倒下豆腐乾絲同炒。
5. 待豆腐乾有香氣時，加調味料調味，再放下肉絲及毛豆，拌炒均勻便可盛出。

＊如果喜食辣味，可酌加紅辣椒絲或辣椒醬同炒。

Ingredients：
240g. dried bean curd, 80g. pork, 2T. fresh soy bean, 3 stalks green onion

Seasonings：
（1）1t. soy sauce, 1t, cornstarch, 1/2T. water
（2）1T. soy sauce, 1/2t. sugar, 1/3t. salt, 3T. water

Procedures：
1. Slice the dried bean curd, then shred it into strings. Boil for 1 minute.
2. Shred the pork, marinate with seasonings (2) for 5 minutes；cut green onions into pieces 1.5cm long.
3. Cook the fresh soy beans for 2 minutes. Rinse with cold water.
4. Heat the wok. Stir-fry the pork with 4T. oil. Drain the pork. Stir-fry the green onion for 10 seconds then add bean curd strings.
5. When the dried bean curd fragrant, season with soy sauce, sugar, and salt. Return the pork and soy beans to the wok, stir-fry thoroughly. Remove to a serving plate.

＊**You may also add red chili or hot bean paste when stir-frying this dish.**

蝦仁豆腐
Bean Curd with Shrimp

材料：
蝦仁2兩、嫩豆腐（6公分四方）4塊、青豆1大匙、蔥花1大匙

調味料：
（1）鹽少許、太白粉半茶匙
（2）鹽1/2茶匙、清湯2/3杯、太白粉水1/2大匙

做法：
1. 蝦仁抽去腸砂，先用鹽抓洗再用冷水沖乾淨，瀝去水分、並用紙巾擦乾，加調味料（1）拌勻，醃5分鐘以上。
2. 嫩豆腐每塊先對切後，再切成1.5公分寬之薄片，全部用開水川燙一下，便可撈出。
3. 用3大匙油先將蝦仁炒過，至蝦仁變白即可撈出。用剩下的油來爆香蔥花，放下豆腐輕輕煎炒，淋下清湯，加鹽調味，放下蝦仁，用小火燒約2分鐘，加入青豆並且用少許之太白粉水勾芡，盛裝盤內。

Ingredients：
120g. shrimp (peeled), 4 pieces soft bean curd (6cm×6cm), 1T. green peas, 1T. chopped green onion

Seasonings：
(1) a little of salt, 1/2t. cornstarch
(2) 1/2t. salt, 2/3C. soup stock, 1/2T. cornstarch paste

Procedures：
1. Rinse shrimp and pat dry. Marinate with seasonings (1) for 5 minutes.
2. Cut the bean curd into 1.5cm wide pieces. Boil for 10 seconds. Drain off the water.
3. Heat 3T. oil to stir-fry shrimp, remove when it is done. Stir-fry green onion with remaining oil. Add bean curd and carefully stir-fry. Add soup stock, salt, and shrimp. Cook over low heat for 2 minutes. Add green peas, thicken with cornstarch paste and serve.

脆皮炸豆腐
Crispy Bean Curd

材料：
嫩豆腐（6公分四方）2塊、太白粉1杯、發泡粉1 1/2茶匙
調味料：
大蒜末1茶匙、醬油膏1大匙、清湯或水1大匙、
甜辣醬1大匙
做法：
1. 將豆腐每塊都切成6小塊（先直切為2塊後，再橫切二刀成為6塊，約3公分四方大小）。
2. 大碗中將太白粉與發泡粉混合均勻，再將豆腐塊放入，輕輕拌勻。
3. 油燒熱後，投下豆腐，用大火炸約1分半鐘，至表面呈金黃色而酥硬時，便可撈出，瀝乾油後，盛入盤中。
4. 附上大蒜醬油膏或甜辣醬或其他喜愛的沾醬上桌，以便沾食。

Ingredients：
2 pieces soft bean curd (6cm×6cm), 1C. cornstarch, 1 1/2 t. baking powder
Seasonings：
1t. chopped garlic, 1T. soy sauce paste,
1T. water or soup stock, 1T. sweet and spicy sauce
Procedures：
1. Cut each piece of bean curd into 6 small cubes (each piece will be about 3cm×3cm).
2. Place cornstarch and baking powder in a large bowl. Add bean curd and mix well.
3. Heat the oil. Deep-fry the bean curd over high heat for about 1 1/2 minutes until the bean curd becomes crispy and golden brown. Drain and place on a platter.
4. Serve with garlic soy sauce mixture (mix garlic, soy sauce paste and water) or sweet and spicy sauce or any sauce you like.

燒豆腐包
Stewed Bean Curd Package

材料：
老豆腐4塊、香菇3朵、筍半個、蛋2個、豆腐衣5張

調味料：
(1) 鹽1/2茶匙、麻油2茶匙
(2) 醬油2大匙、糖1茶匙、水5大匙、麻油少許

做法：
1. 老豆腐放入開水中煮15分鐘後撈出，待涼後，放在白布中搓碎並擠乾水分，將布內之豆腐泥倒出在大碗中。
2. 香菇泡軟後與煮熟之筍子分別剁碎；蛋打散，用少許油炒熟後亦剁碎。全部與豆腐泥一起加調味料（1）拌勻。
3. 豆腐衣每張切成對半，在每小張內放1大匙之豆腐泥料，捲好並打結、紮妥（用少許麵糊封口）。
4. 鍋中燒熱3大匙油，將豆腐包一一排入鍋中，微微煎黃後，淋下調味料（2），蓋上鍋蓋煮約3分鐘，至僅剩下少許湯汁便可裝盤（可撒上熟毛豆數粒點綴）。

Ingredients:
4 pieces hard bean curd (6cm×6cm), 3 black mushrooms, 1/2 bamboo shoot, 2 eggs, 5 pieces dried soy bean sheets

Seasonings:
(1) 1/2t. salt, 2t. sesame oil
(2) 2T. soy sauce, 1t. sugar, 5T. water, seasame oil

Procedures:
1. Boil the bean curd for 15 minutes. Drain and cool. Place in a piece of cheesecloth, smash, and squeeze the excess moisture out. Put the bean curd into a large bowl.
2. Soak the black mushrooms and chop it；cook and chop the bamboo shoot. Beat the eggs, stir-fry and chop. Place all the ingredients in the bowl with the bean curd. Add seasonings (1), mix well.
3. Halve each dried soy bean sheet. Place 1T. of the bean curd mixture on top. Roll and tie the two ends together. Sealing them with flour paste.
4. Heat 3T. oil, fry the bean curd packages. Add seasonings (2), cover and cook for 3 minutes until the liquid is reduced. Sprinkle with sesame oil and serve. (Add some green peas for color)

蛋、豆腐類

110

三鮮烘蛋
Omelet, Chinese Style

材料：
絞肉2大匙、蝦仁2大匙、香菇2朵、蔥屑1大匙、芹菜屑1大匙、蛋6個

調味料：
（1）鹽1/2茶匙、太白粉1茶匙、水1大匙
（2）醬油1/2大匙、鹽1/2茶匙、糖1/2茶匙、水1/2杯、太白粉水2茶匙、麻油少許

做法：
1. 將蛋在大碗中打散，加入調味料（1），用力打鬆至發泡為止。
2. 鍋燒熱後加入1杯油，將蛋汁倒下，蓋下鍋蓋，用小火慢慢烘煎約3分鐘（應時常轉動鍋子，使蛋烘得均勻），見蛋汁已半熟而泡起時，傾斜鍋子將油慢慢倒出，然後將蛋翻轉一面，再烘3分鐘。
3. 見蛋汁已凝固並鬆發時，便可滑出到菜板上，馬上切成5公分長、3公分寬大小，排在盤中。
4. 另用2大匙油先將絞肉及蔥屑炒熟，再加入已炒過之蝦仁丁和香菇（泡軟、切小丁），並用醬油、鹽、糖調味，加入水2/3杯，煮滾後用太白粉水勾芡，淋下麻油，撒下芹菜屑便可澆在蛋上上桌。

Ingredients：
2T. ground pork, 2T. shrimp (peeled), 2 black mushrooms, 1T. chopped green onion, 1T. chopped celery, 6 eggs

Seasonings：
（1）$1/2$ t. salt, 1t. cornstarch, 1T. water
（2）$1/2$ T. soy sauce, $1/2$t. salt, $1/2$t.sugar, $1/2$C. water, 2t.cornstarch paste, sesame oil

Procedures：
1. Beat the eggs in a large bowl. Add seasonings (1). Beat until puffy.
2. Heat 1C. oil in a wok. Pour the eggs in and cover the wok. Fry over low heat for about 3 minutes until golden brown on the bottom, then turn the egg omelet over.
3. When the eggs become firm and completely done (about 3 minutes), remove and cut into pieces 3×5cm. Place on a platter.
4. Stir-fry ground pork and green onion with 2T. oil. Add shrimp and diced black mushrooms. Season with soy sauce, salt, and sugar. Add $2/3$C. water and bring to a boil. Thicken with cornstarch paste. Sprinkle with sesame oil and celery. Pour the sauce over the eggs and serve quickly.

*烘蛋屬四川名菜，有魚香味的、屑子料的、蝦仁的、火腿的、白油等許多不同味道的澆頭。

* **This kind of egg omelet is very famous in Sze- chuan, you may use different sauce to change the flavor.**

蛋、豆腐類

番茄炒蛋
Stir-fried Eggs with Tomato

材料：
番茄2個、蛋4個、蔥花1大匙

調味料：
鹽2/3茶匙、糖1茶匙

做法：
1. 在番茄的頂端用刀子輕劃十字刀口，放在開水中燙約1分鐘，至番茄皮脫落，便可撈出。將皮剝淨，切成3公分四方大小，將番茄子與瓤儘量擠出不用。
2. 蛋4個加鹽1/3茶匙打散，至無塊粒為止。
3. 鍋燒熱後放油3大匙，將蛋炒至八分熟盛出。另用2大匙油將蔥花爆香，放進番茄大火炒片刻，加鹽與糖調味，並加入3大匙水，再倒下炒好之蛋一同拌炒均勻，即可裝盤。

Ingredients：
2 tomatoes, 4 eggs, 1T. chopped green onion

Seasonings：
2/3t. salt, 1t. sugar

Procedures：
1. Score the top of the tomatoes. Boil for 1 minute until the skin peels off. Remove the skin and cut the tomatoes into 3cm cubes. Squeeze the seeds out.
2. Beat the 4 eggs with 1/3t. salt.
3. Heat 3T. oil to stir-fry eggs until almost done. Remove. Heat another 2T. oil to stir-fry the green onions, add tomatoes and stir-fry over high heat for 20 seconds. Season with salt and sugar. Pour the eggs back into the wok and stir-fry thoroughly. Remove to a plate.

碎肉蒸蛋
Steamed Eggs with Minced Pork

材料：
蛋3個、絞肉2兩、蔥花2大匙

調味料：
醬油1/2大匙、鹽1/2茶匙、水1/2杯

做法：

1. 蔥花與絞肉一起放在砧板上，再剁片刻，同放在深盤或麵碗中，將蛋3個加入，再一同打散，打至蛋白完全散開無塊粒時，加調味料拌攪均勻。
2. 打好的碎肉及蛋放入蒸鍋或電鍋中，蒸約20~25分鐘，至完全凝固時便可取出上桌。

* 蒸蛋的老與嫩完全決定在加水的多少與火候的大小，一般蒸蛋的水的比例是與蛋一樣多，如要嫩些可將水加倍，再以小火慢慢地蒸。

Ingredients：
3 eggs, 80g. ground pork, 2T. chopped green onion

Seasonings：
1/2T. soy sauce, 1/2t. salt, 1/2C. water

Procedures：

1. Chop the ground pork and green onion. Place in a large bowl (or a deep plate). Beat 3 eggs together in the same bowl until smooth. Add soy sauce, salt, and water. Mix thoroughly.
2. Steam for about 20~25 minutes until done and serve.

* Generally, when you make steamed egg dish, you use the same proportion of egg and water. If you want the eggs to be very soft, you should add more water and steam over low heat.

蛋、豆腐類

麵拖老蛋
Deep-fried Boiled Egg with Clear Sauce

材料：
蛋4個
調味料：
醬油2大匙、糖2茶匙、水6大匙
麵糊料： 麵粉4大匙、水2/3杯
做法：
1. 將蛋放入清水中煮10分鐘至蛋已完全煮熟（成為老蛋），浸過冷水，待其涼後，剝去蛋殼，將蛋橫切為4塊。
2. 碗中將麵糊料調好。
3. 在鍋中將炸油燒熱，放下沾了麵糊的蛋塊油炸，炸至外表呈金黃色而酥脆時，撈出。
4. 另在鍋內放入調味料，煮滾後，用剩餘之麵糊倒入勾芡，使汁變得濃稠，再把炸好之老蛋倒下，快速略加拌合，盛出裝盤。

Ingredients：
4 eggs
Seasonings：
2T. soy sauce, 2t. sugar, 6T. water
Flour batter： 4T. flour, 2/3C. water
Proceduress：
1. Boil the eggs for 10 minutes, soak in cold water. Remove shells when it cool. Cut each egg into 4 pieces.
2. Combine 4T. flour and 8T. water into a flour paste. Coat eggs with the flour paste.
3. Deep-fry the eggs until golden brown and crispy. Remove and drain off oil.
4. Boil the seasonings. Thicken with remaining flour paste. Turn off the heat. Return the eggs to the wok. Mix and serve.

紅燒蛋餃
Stewed Egg Dumplings with Vegetable

材料：
絞肉4兩、蔥1支、蛋5個、大白菜1/2斤、粉絲1小把

調味料：
（1）酒1茶匙、醬油1茶匙、太白粉1茶匙
（2）醬油2大匙、鹽1/2茶匙、清湯或水1杯

做法：

1. 蔥切成屑後，與絞肉一起剁過，放入大碗中，加調味料（1）仔細拌勻。蛋打散過篩一次備用。

2. 炒菜鍋燒熱，改成小火。在鍋之中間塗上少許油料，放入1大匙的蛋汁，轉動鍋子，使蛋汁成為橢圓形之薄餅狀。在中央放入1/2大匙的肉餡，並將蛋皮覆蓋過來，稍微壓住，使蛋皮周圍密合，略煎10秒鐘，翻面再煎5秒，便可盛出即是蛋餃。全部做好留用。

3. 大白菜洗淨、切成3公分寬、6公分長。在鍋中用4大匙油炒軟，放下調味料（2），將蛋餃放在白菜上，以小火煮15分鐘，加入泡軟之粉絲，再燒一下至湯汁收乾一點，便可裝盤。

Ingredients:
150 ground pork, 1 stalk green onion, 5 eggs, 300g. Chinese cabbage, 1 bundle mung bean threads

Seasonings:
(1) 1t. wine, 1t. soy sauce, 1t. cornstarch
(2) 2T. soy sauce, 1/2t. salt, 1C. soup or water

Procedures:

1. Chop the pork and green onion. Place in a large bowl. Add seasonings (1), mix well. Beat the egg until smooth.

2. Heat the wok and rub some oil in the center. Make a small pancake by placing 1 T. of the beaten egg mixture in the wok. Place 1/2T. of the meat on top of the egg. Fold the pancake in half, slightly pressing it to seal the egg. Fry over low heat for 10 seconds. Turn it over and fry for another 5 seconds. Remove. Make all the egg dumplings.

3. Trim and cut the Chinese cabbage into 3cm×6cm pieces. Stir-fry with 2T. oil until soft. Add seasonings (2). Place egg dumplings on cabbage. Simmer for 15 minutes. Add soaked bean threads. Cook for 2 minutes until the liquid is almost absorbed. Serve.

蔬菜類

116

糖醋蓮白捲
Sweet & Sour Cabbage Rolls

材料：

高麗菜1棵、香菇絲2大匙、火腿絲2大匙、芹菜2支、綠豆芽4兩、花椒粒1大匙

調味料：

（1）糖4大匙、醋4大匙、醬油2大匙
（2）鹽1/4茶匙、麻油1茶匙

做法：

1. 炒鍋內燒開6杯水，加少許鹽，將高麗菜整棵放進水中燙軟，剝下6大片菜葉，並削除少許硬梗。
2. 在大碗中，將調味料（1）混合，放下高麗菜葉浸泡30分鐘（需時常翻動）。
3. 芹菜切成3公分長；豆芽摘好洗淨，兩種均放入開水中燙片刻、至脫生後即撈出。擠乾水分與香菇絲、火腿絲同裝一碗內，拌少許鹽和麻油。
4. 浸過汁的高麗菜葉，每兩片相接。將豆芽等在中間排成一字形，緊緊捲成筒狀。捲好後再切成3公分長，排在盤內。
5. 鍋內用油將花椒炸香，馬上撈棄，再將泡高麗菜所剩的汁倒入煮滾，盛出。待涼後淋到蓮白捲上即可上桌。

Ingredients：

1 cabbage, 2T. shredded black mushroom, 2 stalks celery, 150g. bean sprouts, 1T. brown peppercorn

Seasonings：

（1）4T. sugar, 4T. vinegar, 2T. soy sauce
（2）1/4t. salt, 1t. sesame oil

Procedures：

1. Boil 6C. water in wok. Add a little of salt. Boil the whole cabbage until soft. Remove and save 6 leaves from the outer part of the cabbage. Trim the leaves thinner.
2. In a large bowl, mix seasonings (1). Soak the cabbage leaves in the juice for 1/2 hour (turn them over often).
3. Cut the celery into pieces 3cm long; trim and rinse the bean sprouts. Boil both for about 30 seconds. Drain and squeeze out the excess water. Place the celery, bean sprouts, black mushrooms, and ham in a bowl. Add seasonings (2), mix well.
4. Place two cabbage leaves together (arrange them in a rectangular shape). Place 1/3 of #3 mixture in the middle. Roll and fold tightly. Cut the roll into pieces 3cm long. Arrange on a platter. Make the other 2 rolls.
5. Fry brown peppercorn with 2T. oil. Discard the peppercorn. Add the liquid (remaining from the soaked cabbage). Bring to a boil. Pour the sauce over the cabbage rolls when they cool. Serve.

酸辣黃瓜
Hot & Sour Cucumbers

材料：
小黃瓜1½斤、大蒜10粒、紅辣椒3支、花椒粒1大匙

調味料：
醋4大匙、糖4大匙、鹽½茶匙

做法：
1. 選新鮮的黃瓜，先切成約5公分長，再對剖為兩半，挖去中間瓜子，（除去瓜子黃瓜才會脆）；大蒜拍碎；紅辣椒切小段。
2. 鍋中燒熱3大匙油，放下大蒜、紅辣椒段及花椒（如不喜辣者，則紅辣椒留至最後才放），爆炒至有香氣透出，放下黃瓜片，隨即放下調味料，拌炒數下，煮滾約半分鐘後熄火。
3. 將黃瓜連汁裝入一只大碗中，蓋上一個盤子，讓黃瓜燜至涼透，便可放在冰箱中，隨吃隨取。

  ＊本菜是一道酸甜、爽口、開胃的小菜，冰後更加好吃。

  ＊**This is a delicious appetizer. It tastes even better when it is cold.**

Ingredients：
2 lb. small cucumbers, 10 cloves garlic, 3 red chilies, 1T. brown peppercorn

Seasonings：
4T. vinegar, 4T. sugar, ½t. salt

Procedures：
1. Cut the small cucumbers into pieces 5cm long, then halve it. Remove the seeds；crush the garlic；dice the red pepper.
2. Heat 3T. oil. Fry the garlic, red chili, and brown peppercorn (if you don't want this dish too spicy, you may add the red pepper at last). When fragrant, add the cucumber and seasonings. Stir-fry and let it boil for ½ minute. Turn off the heat.
3. Pour the cucumbers and sauce into a large bowl. Cover until it cools. Reserve in a jar. This dish will keep for up to a week.

拌海蜇皮
Jellyfish Salad

材料：

海蜇皮3兩、大白菜心半棵（約4兩）、胡蘿蔔絲1/2杯、乾蝦米2大匙、香菜段2大匙、大蒜泥1/2大匙

調味料：

醬油3大匙、醋2大匙、糖1/2茶匙、麻油1大匙

做法：

1. 海蜇皮捲緊成筒狀，切成細絲。放大碗內用冷水泡上3小時。放入開水內快速燙約3~5秒鐘，立刻撈出，再放回大碗中泡半天以上（要時常換水才會脹胖）。
2. 大白菜剖開洗淨，將每葉先切成6公分寬的段，再直紋切成細絲（太厚的地方須先片開）；胡蘿蔔切成4公分長細絲；香菜切3公分長；蝦米用溫水泡軟，除去頭腳。
3. 大蒜泥放入碗中，加調味料調勻。
4. 海蜇絲及所有材料等放入大碗中，加調味汁拌勻便可裝盤。

Ingredients：

150g. jellyfish, 150g. Chinese cabbage, 1/2C. shredded carrot, 2T. dried shrimp, 2T. cilantro section, 1/2T. smashed garlic

Seasonings：

3T. soy sauce, 2T. vinegar, 1/2t. sugar, 1T. sesame oil

Procedures：

1. Roll the jellyfish, shred it into thin strings. Soak in cold water for 3 hours. Place in a strainer and blanch it into boiling water for 3~5 seconds. Soak in cold water for half a day (change the water 3 or 4 times).
2. Shred the Chinese cabbage into thin strings 6cm long；shred the carrot 4cm long; cut he parsley into 3cm long；soak the dried shrimp in warm water for 10 minutes, remove the heads and feet.
3. Mix garlic and the seasonings well.
4. Mix jellyfish and all ingredients with the seasoning, mix evenly and serve.

蔬菜類

蔬菜類

芥末拌洋芹
Celery Salad with Mustard

材料：
西洋芹菜1/2斤

調味料：
(1) 鹽1/2茶匙、糖1大匙
(2) 芥末粉1 1/2大匙、冷開水1 1/2大匙、麻油2大匙、醋1茶匙

做法：
1. 將芹菜一支支由根部折下，再將每支上之硬筋撕下後，全部切成約5公分長段（也可用手折短）。
2. 燒半鍋開水（水中加鹽1/2茶匙），投下全部芹菜，大火燙煮約15~20秒鐘，撈出後沖過冷水，再在冰水中浸泡約5~10分鐘。
3. 瀝乾芹菜、並用紙巾拭去水分，加入鹽及糖拌勻，醃15分鐘後再瀝乾汁液。
4. 芥末粉用冷開水調稀，加入麻油、醋，再仔細調拌成膏狀，澆到芹菜中，反覆調拌，裝到碟中即可供食。

Ingredients：
300g. celery

Seasonings：
(1) 1/2t. salt, 1T. sugar
(2) 1 1/2T. mustard powder, 1 1/2T. cold water, 2T. sesame oil, 1t. vinegar

Procedures：
1. Peel off the celery skin, cut into 5cm long stripes.
2. Boil the celery over high heat for 20 seconds. Drain and rinse with cold water, soak in ice water for 5~10 minutes.
3. Drain the celery and pat dry with paper towel. Mix with salt and sugar, soak for 15 minutes. Drain again.
4. Mix mustard powder and water in a small bowl. Add sesame oil and vinegar. Mix thoroughly to form a paste consistency. Pour over the celery. Mix again. Transfer to a plate and serve.

炒肉絲拉皮
Stir-fried Pork with Salad

材料：
全瘦豬肉3兩、小黃瓜1條、新鮮粉皮1疊、蔥絲半杯

調味料：
（1）醬油½大匙、太白粉1茶匙、水1大匙
（2）芥末粉1大匙、冷開水2大匙、芝麻醬1大匙、醬油1大匙、醋1大匙、麻油1大匙、鹽少許

做法：
1. 豬肉切細絲，用調味料（1）拌醃10分鐘，用七分熱之油過油炒熟，再同蔥絲合炒一下，盛出。
2. 小黃瓜洗淨、擦乾，連皮切成細絲，放在碟中；新鮮粉皮切成6公分長、1.5公分寬之條狀，堆在黃瓜之上，再將肉絲撒在粉皮上面。
3. 芥末粉和芝麻醬分別用冷開水調開，再和其他的調味料（2）調勻。和肉絲一起上桌，臨食前淋下、拌勻。

Ingredients:
120g. lean pork, 1 cucumber, 1 piece mung bean sheet, 1/2C. shredded green onion

Seasonings:
（1） ½T. soy sauce, 1t. cornstarch, 1T. water
（2） 1T. mustard powder, 2T. drinking water, 1T. sesame paste, 1T. soy sauce, 1T. vinegar, 1T. sesame oil, a little of salt

Procedures:
1. shred the pork, marinate with seasonings (1) for 5 minutes. Stir-fry in 2T. oil. When the pork is done, add shredded green onion in and mix them.
2. Shred the small cucumber. Place on a plate. Cut the fresh mung bean sheets into pieces 6cm long × 1.5cm wide. Place on top of the cucumber, then put the pork on top of the bean sheets.
3. Mix mustard powder with water, and sesame seed paste with soy sauce in two different bowls. Mix the two sauces together and add vinegar, sesame oil, and salt. Mix thoroughly. Pour the sauce over the meat mixture just before eating. Mix well.

魚香溜茄夾
Stuffed Eggplants, Sze-chuan Style

材料：

茄子2條、絞豬肉半斤、蔥屑2茶匙、薑屑1茶匙、蒜屑1茶匙

蛋麵糊料： 蛋1個、麵粉3大匙、太白粉3大匙、水適量

調味料：

（1）蔥屑1/2大匙、薑汁1茶匙、醬油1/2大匙、鹽1/4茶匙、太白粉1茶匙、酒1茶匙

（2）辣豆瓣醬1大匙、醬油1大匙、太白粉1茶匙、糖1茶匙、醋1茶匙、酒1茶匙、鹽1/4茶匙、麻油少許、清水4大匙

做法：

1. 茄子由尖頭處斜著切雙飛片，要切一刀連、一刀斷。在夾縫中抹一點太白粉。
2. 將絞肉再剁碎，盛在大碗中，加入調味料（1）拌勻，然後分別塞入茄子夾縫中。
3. 蛋打散，加其他的麵糊料，調成糊狀。
4. 油燒熱，投下沾蛋麵糊的茄夾，用中火炸成金黃色。
5. 在鍋內燒熱2大匙油，爆炒辣豆瓣醬及蔥薑蒜屑，並倒下其他的調味料（2），拌炒至稠後熄火，放進茄子夾混合，馬上裝盤上桌。

Ingredients：

2 Chinese eggplants, 300g. ground pork, 2t. chopped green onion, 1t. chopped ginger, 1t. chopped garlic

Flour batter： 1 egg, 3T. flour, 3T. cornstarch, water

Seasonings：

（1）1/2T. chopped green onion, 1t. ginger juice, 1/2T. soysauce, 1/4t. salt, 1t. cornstarch, 1t. wine

（2）1T. hot bean paste, 1T. soy sauce, 1t. cornstarch, 1t. sugar, 1t. vinegar, 1t. wine, 1/4t. salt, sesame oil, 4T. water

Procedures：

1. Cut the eggplant diagonally, slice the eggplant into pieces 1cm thick. Slice each piece again in half—but DO NOT cut all the way through. Sprinkle some cornstarch in between.
2. Mix ground pork with seasonings (1) in a bowl. Stuff into the eggplant.
3. Beat the egg to make flour batter.
4. Coat the stuffed eggplant with flour batter. Deep-fry in hot oil over medium heat. Drain the eggplant after it done and golden brown.
5. Stir-fry the hot bean paste, green onion, ginger, and garlic with 2T. oil, add other seasonings (2). Bring to a boil, turn off the heat. Add eggplant in, mix quickly and remove.

肉末四季豆
String Beans with Pork

材料：
四季豆12兩、絞肉2兩、粉絲1把、蔥屑1大匙

調味料：
醬油1大匙、鹽1/2茶匙、糖1/4茶匙、水1杯、麻油少許

做法：

1. 選用較短扁而翠綠之嫩四季豆，摘去兩端及兩邊之硬筋，每根折成兩半。
2. 在鍋內將4大匙油燒至極熱，放下四季豆用大火煸炒，至四季豆變軟後盛出（約3分鐘）。
3. 鍋中另燒油2大匙，放下絞肉炒散，再加入蔥屑同炒片刻，淋下醬油、鹽、糖及水，放下四季豆同燒約3分鐘。
4. 加入泡軟之粉絲，再燒煮2~3分鐘，改大火將湯汁收乾，淋下麻油少許便可裝盤。

Ingredients：
450g. string beans, 80g. ground pork, 1bundle bean threads, 1T. chopped green onion,

Seasonings：
1T. Soy sauce, 1/2t. salt, 1/4t. sugar, 1/2C. water, a few drops sesame oil

Procedures：

1. Choose tender string beans. Trim and cut beans in half.
2. Heat 4T. oil in wok. Stir-fry the string beans over high heat for about 3 minutes. Remove when the beans become soft (about 3 minutes).
3. Use another 2T. oil to stir-fry the ground pork. Add green onion and stir-fry together. Season with seasonings (except sesame oil), boil for 3 minutes.
4. Add bean threads (already soaked in warm water for 20 minutes) and cook until soft, reduce the liquid over high heat. Sprinkle with sesame oil and transfer to a plate.

雪菜炒肉絲
Stir-fried Pork with Mustard Green

材料：
雪裡紅4兩、肉絲3兩、百頁6張、
鹼1/2茶匙或小蘇打1/4茶匙、蔥花1大匙

調味料：
（1）醬油1茶匙、太白粉1茶匙、水1大匙
（2）鹽少許、糖少許

做法：
1. 雪裡紅洗淨，擠乾水份。一支支撕開並將尾梢之葉子部分切除，莖部切成細片狀（碎屑）備用。
2. 豬肉切絲後用調味料（1）醃10分鐘。
3. 百頁切1公分寬條，用熱鹼水（3杯熱水中加1粒花生米大小之鹼塊或小蘇打粉1/4茶匙）泡至變色。撈出再用冷水漂洗乾淨備用。
4. 鍋中燒熱3大匙油，放下蔥花爆香，再放肉絲炒熟，加雪裡紅及百頁下鍋拌炒，並加鹽和糖調味，炒透便可盛出。

＊百頁不易買到的話，可以不用，亦可以加筍絲同炒。

＊**You may use shredded bamboo shoots instead of bean curd sheets.**

Ingredients：
150g. preserved mustard green, 120g. pork strings, 6 pieces bean curd sheets, 1/4t. baking soda, 2C. hot water, 1T. chopped green onion

Seasonings：
（1）1t. soy sauce, 1t. cornstarch, 1T. water
（2）salt and sugar

Procedures：
1. Rinse and squeeze the salted vegetable. Chop into small pieces.
2. Marinate pork string with seasonings (1).
3. Cut the bean curd sheets into strings 1cm wide. Soak in 3C. hot water (add 1/4 t. baking soda) until the color turns light. Drain and rinse with water.
4. Heat 3T. oil, stir-fry green onion and pork. Add mustard green and bean curd sheets. Season with salt and sugar. Stir-fry thoroughly, then remove to a plate.

素炒十香菜
Stir-fried Assorted Vegetables

材料：

香菇4朵、筍1支、榨菜2兩、胡蘿蔔2支、豆腐乾4塊、醬瓜2兩、芹菜4兩、黃豆芽4兩

調味料：

鹽少許、糖少許、麻油2大匙

做法：

1. 香菇用冷水泡軟後去蒂；筍煮熟，撈出後沖過冷水，切細絲；榨菜洗後切細絲；醬瓜、胡蘿蔔和豆腐乾均分別切絲。
2. 用2大匙油將豆芽先炒軟，再加入芹菜同炒，隨即盛出。
3. 再以麻油將香菇絲和胡蘿蔔絲至炒軟，加入筍絲、榨菜絲、豆腐乾絲、醬瓜絲等材料繼續炒香，加鹽、糖調味，一起炒勻。然後將黃豆芽、芹菜倒入與前項各料拌勻，即可裝盤。

Ingredients：

4 black mushrooms, 1 bamboo shoot, 80g. preserved mustard, 1/2 carrot, 4 pieces dried bean curd, 80g. pickled cucumber, 150g. celery, 150g. Soy bean sprouts

Seasonings：

Salt, sugar, 2T. sesame oil

Procedures：

1. Shred the soaked black mushrooms; Cook and shred the bamboo shoot; shred the preserved mustard, pickled cucumber, carrot and dried bean curd.
2. Heat 2T. oil to stir-fry soybean sprouts until it turns soft. Add celery and stir-fry for 1 minute more. Remove.
3. Heat 2T. sesame oil, stir-fry black mushrooms and carrot, when it fragrant, add bamboo shoots, preserved mustard, dried bean curd, and pickled cucumber over high heat. Stir-fry thoroughly. Add soybean sprouts and celery, season with salt, sugar. Stir well and serve.

蔬菜類

干貝鮮筍衣
Slice Bamboo Shoots with Dried Scallop

材料：
綠竹筍4支、干貝1兩、熱水1杯、雞湯3杯、蔥屑少許、薑末少許

調味料：
鹽酌量、酒酌量、太白粉水1大匙

做法：
1. 將干貝用熱水泡半小時後，再蒸半小時。待稍冷後，用手撕成細絲備用。
2. 筍去皮、煮熟後，削掉底部老的部分。先直剖兩半，再順絲切成極薄之片狀。用2杯雞湯以小火煨煮10分鐘撈出。
3. 起油鍋先爆香蔥、薑，淋酒、加入雞湯1杯與蒸干貝之湯汁（約1/2杯）煮滾，放下筍片與干貝，並加鹽調味，用小火煨煮5分鐘左右。
4. 淋下調水之太白粉勾芡成糊狀，裝盤即可。

* 綠竹筍清而爽口，在夏季更是美味，配上海味烹煮可做宴客菜，家常可改用蝦米同燴。

* You may use dried shrimp instead of dried scallop.

Ingredients：
4 bamboo shoots, 40g. dried scallops, 4C. chicken stock, 1T. chopped green onion, 1/2t. chopped ginger

Seasonings：
salt, wine, 1T. cornstarch paste

Procedures：
1. Soak the dried scallops with hot water 1/2 hour. Steam for 1/2 hour. Separate the scallops while it cools.
2. Cook the peeled bamboo shoots. Cut in half, then slice it to very thin slices. Cook with 2C. chicken stock for 10 minutes. Drain.
3. Stir-fry green onions and ginger with 2T. oil. Sprinkle with wine, add 1C. chicken stock and the liquid from the steamed scallops (about 1/2 cup). Bring to a boil. Add bamboo shoots and scallops. Season with some salt. Simmer for 5 minutes.
4. Thicken with cornstarch paste. Transfer to a large platter.

醬燒茄子
Eggplants with Sweet Soybean Paste

材料：
茄子3條、絞肉2大匙、蔥屑1大匙、蒜屑1大匙

調味料：
甜麵醬（或豆瓣醬）1大匙、醬油1大匙、糖½大匙、水3大匙、鎮江醋½大匙、麻油½茶匙

做法：

1. 選購色澤光亮、新鮮的茄子，切成5公分長段，再直剖成長條，泡入鹽水中，下鍋前瀝乾水分。
2. 鍋中5大匙油先燒熱，放下茄子大火煸炒至茄子軟透、無硬心時就撈起，瀝出。
3. 另用2大匙油將絞肉與蒜屑爆香，放下甜麵醬再炒片刻、至醬香溢出，便可加醬油、糖及水炒勻，將茄子落鍋拌炒，改小火燒煮2分鐘，至汁已收乾，便可淋下醋及麻油，撒下蔥粒即裝上盤。

Ingredients:
3 eggplants, 2T. ground pork, 1T. chopped green onion, 1T. chopped garlic

Seasonings:
1T. sweet soybean paste, 1T. soy sauce, ½t. sugar, 3T. water, ½T. vinegar, ½t. sesame oil

Procedures:

1. Cut the eggplants into strips 5cm long × 1cm wide. Soak in salty water for 5 minutes, drain before stir-frying.
2. Heat 5T. oil in wok, stir-fry eggplant until soft. Drain.
3. Heat 2T. oil to stir-fry pork and garlic. Add soybean paste. Stir-fry over low heat. When fragrant, add soy sauce, sugar, and water. Add the eggplant in. Cook over low heat for 2 minutes, until the liquid is absorbed. Sprinkle with vinegar, sesame oil, and green onion. Remove to the plate.

* 若要保持茄子的紫色，可用較多量的熱油，大火炸30秒，撈出再燒。

* You may deep-fry the eggplant in hot oil for 30 seconds to keep the purple color.

醋烹銀芽
Quick Stir-fried Bean Sprouts

材料：
綠豆芽半斤、豌豆莢絲半杯、紅辣椒1支、香菇2朵、嫩薑絲1/3杯

材料：
（1）鹽1/3茶匙
（2）糖1大匙、醋3大匙、麻油2茶匙

做法：
1. 綠豆牙洗淨、瀝乾；香菇泡軟、切絲；紅辣椒去子、切絲。
2. 將2大匙油燒熱，放下綠豆芽及豌豆莢絲同炒約20秒鐘，瀝出。
3. 另用2大匙油炒香香菇絲，炒透後加入薑絲和紅辣椒，並再落第一項之豆芽，加鹽，大火拌炒，馬上淋下預備在碗中之糖醋料，大火鏟拌均勻即裝碟。

Ingredients：
300g. bean sprouts, 1/2C. shredded snow pea pots, 2 red chili, 2 black mushrooms, 1/3 C. shredded black mushrooms

Seasonings：
(1) 1/3t. salt
(2) 1T. sugar, 3T. vinegar, 2t. sesame oil

Procedure：
1. Trim bean sprouts；soak black mushrooms to soft, shred it；remove seeds from red chili, shred it.
2. Heat 2T. oil to stir-fry bean sprouts and shredded snow pea pot for 20 seconds. Drain.
3. Heat 2T. oil to stir-fry black mushroom, when fragrant, add ginger and red chili. Add bean sprouts and salt, sprinkle with seasonings (2), stir-fry thoroughly, then serve.

三絲空心菜
Stir-fried Water Convolvulus

材料：
五香豆腐乾4塊、空心菜半斤、木耳絲半杯、
紅辣椒1支、大蒜2粒

調味料：
沙茶醬2茶匙、醬油2茶匙、糖1/2茶匙、鹽1/3茶匙、
水1大匙

做法：
1. 空心菜摘成約7公分長度，洗淨、瀝乾；豆腐乾切絲；紅辣椒去子、切絲；大蒜剁碎。
2. 小碗中將調味料先調勻。鍋中燒熱2大匙油，爆香大蒜末，倒下調味料炒勻，盛出。
3. 燒滾5杯水，放入空心菜、豆腐乾和木耳絲，菜一熟即撈出，和紅椒絲一起放入調味料中拌勻、盛入盤中。

Ingredients：
4 pieces dried bean curd, 300g. water convolvulus, 1/2C. shredded black fungus, 1 red chili, 2 cloves garlic

Seasonings：
2t. sha-cha sauce, 2t. soy sauce, 1/2t. sugar, 1/3t. salt, 2T. water

Procedures：
1. Trim water convolvulus to about 7cm long sections, rinse and drain；shred dried bean curd；remove seeds from red chili, shred it; chop garlic.
2. Mix seasonings in a bowl. Heat 2T. oil to fry the garlic, when fragrant, add seasonings, stir-fry and remove.
3. Boil all ingredients in 5C. water, remove when the water convolvulus turn soft. Mix with the sauce, remove to a plate.

蔬菜類

五味苦瓜
Bitter Gourd with Rich Sauce

材料：
苦瓜1條、蔥屑1大匙、薑屑1茶匙、蒜屑1/2大匙、紅辣椒屑1茶匙

調味料：
麻油1/2大匙、淡色醬油2大匙、糖1/2大匙、鎮江醋1大匙

做法：
1. 苦瓜直剖為四半之後，挖出籽、洗淨，用冷開水泡著（冷開水須蓋過苦瓜），放進冰箱內冰鎮2~3小時，以除去苦瓜的生味。
2. 將蔥、薑、蒜和紅辣椒屑放在小碗中，加入調味料拌勻便是五味汁，可用來沾苦瓜片的。
3. 待要食用時，將苦瓜取出，瀝乾水分，將中央軟肉除去，再切成極薄之片狀，排放在盤中，食時沾五味汁便可（將汁淋下亦可）。

  ＊亦可配美乃滋或千島醬（美乃滋加番茄醬調勻）沾食。

  ＊**You may use the ma-yonnaise or thousand island dressing instead of five spicy sauce.**

Ingredients：
1 bitter gourd, 1T. chopped green onion, 1t. chopped ginger, 1/2T. chopped garlic, 1t. chopped red chili

Seasonings：
1/2T. sesame oil, 2T. light color soy sauce, 1/2T. sugar, 1T. vinegar

Procedures：
1. Cut the bitter gourd lengthwise into 4 pieces. Remove the seeds. Soak in cold water (the water must cover the gourd). Put in refrigerator for 2~3 hours to remove the bitter taste.
2. Place green onion, ginger, garlic, and red chili in a small bowl. Mix with the seasonings. This is the five spice sauce.
3. Before serving, drain the gourd and pat it dry. Remove the soft flesh from the center part. Cut into very thin slices, arrange on a plate. Serve with the sauce. Pour the sauce over the gourd just before eating.

酥肉蒸蘿蔔
Steamed Pork with Radish

材料：
豬前腿肉6兩、白蘿蔔1斤、蕃薯粉1/2杯、2/3杯清湯

醃肉料： 醬油3大匙、紅蔥頭屑或蒜屑1茶匙、
糖1/4茶匙、胡椒粉少許

調味料：
鹽1/2茶匙、蔥屑1大匙

做法：

1. 將豬肉切成如小拇指大小，用醃肉料拌勻，再沾上蕃薯粉、用熱油炸黃且至酥脆為止，撈出裝在碗內。
2. 白蘿蔔也切條狀，用鹽及蔥屑拌勻，鋪在碗內的豬肉上面，淋下1/2杯清湯，上鍋蒸40分鐘。
3. 將一只深底盤蓋在第二項之蒸碗上，先泌出湯汁，再翻扣一下，使酥肉蘿蔔倒扣到盤中，再將湯汁澆回便成。

Ingredients：
240g. lean pork, 600g. radish, 1/2C. sweet potato powder, 2/3C. soup stock

To marinate pork： 3T. soy sauce, 1t. fried red shallot, 1/4t. sugar, a little of pepper

Seasonings：
1/2t. salt, 1T. chopped green onion

Procedures：

1. Cut the pork into stripes 1cm wide × 3cm long. Mix with marinade. Coat with sweet potato powder and deep-fry in hot oil until crispy. Drain and place in a bowl.
2. Cut the radish into stripes 3cm × 1cm. Mix with salt and green onion. Place on top of the pork. Add 1/2C. soup stock. Steam for 40 minutes. Remove.
3. Cover the bowl with a large platter. Drain off and reserve the soup. Turn the bowl over so the pork and radish are now on the platter. Pour the soup back over the pork and serve.

腰片湯
Sliced Kidney Soup

材料：
大豬腰1個、榨菜1兩、豆苗2兩（或嫩豆莢10片）、嫩薑10小片、清湯6杯

調味料：
鹽1茶匙、胡椒粉少許、麻油少許

做法：
1. 將豬腰先橫面剖開，挖除內部白色筋絡後洗淨，再在光面上直劃切七、八條刀紋（要深入腰子的一半厚度），然後橫面切成大斜片（左手指按住豬腰）。
2. 腰子切好後全部泡在冷水中，要多換幾次水，至水清澈、不混濁。榨菜洗去辣椒粉、切成大薄片。
3. 將豆苗摘下嫩葉，洗淨並拭乾水分，裝在大湯碗內。
4. 鍋中燒開半鍋水，投入腰片，以大火燙熟，隨即撈出，瀝去水分，攤平排列在豆苗上，並撒下胡椒粉及麻油。
5. 將清湯或水燒滾，放進榨菜與薑片，同時加入鹽調味，趁大滾時即離火，沖淋到大湯碗中（可燙熟豆苗）便成。

Ingredients：
1 pork kidney, 40g. preserved mustard, 80g. snow pea pots, 10 slices ginger, 6C. soup stock

Seasonings：
1t. salt, a little of pepper and sesame oil

Procedures：
1. Cut the kidney in half horizontally and remove the white membrane. Score 7 or 8 cuts from end to end, about half way through the kidney. Slice into large pieces.
2. Soak the kidney in cold water (change the water several times until the water is clear). Wash the salted vegetables and slice it.
3. Trim and rinse the snow pea pots, pat dry and place in a soup bowl.
4. Boil kidney over high heat. Drain and place on top of snow pea pots. Sprinkle with pepper and sesame oil.
5. Once the soup stock boils, add salted vegetables and ginger. Season with salt. When it boils again, pour into the serving bowl.

酸辣湯
Hot & Sour Soup

材料：

瘦豬肉1塊約3兩、豆腐（6公分四方）1塊、雞血半塊、木耳半杯、筍1支、蛋1個、蔥花少許

調味料：

鹽1茶匙、醬油2大匙、太白粉水3大匙、胡椒粉1茶匙、醋2大匙、麻油1/4大匙

做法：

1. 將瘦豬肉整塊煮20分鐘（用6杯水），取出待冷後，切成細絲。豆腐、雞血、木耳（泡軟）、筍（煮熟）分別切成約5~6公分長細絲，蛋打散備用。
2. 煮肉湯汁煮滾，加入所有材料（蛋除外），加鹽和醬油調味，再滾後即勾芡。改小火，倒入蛋汁。
3. 湯碗中放入胡椒粉、麻油和醋，倒入酸辣湯並撒下蔥花。

Ingredients：

120g. lean pork, 1 piece bean curd (6cm × 6cm), 1/2 piece coagulated chicken blood (optional), 1/2 C. black fungus, 1 bamboo shoot, 1 egg, chopped green onion

Seasonings：

1t. salt, 2T. soy sauce, 3T. cornstarch paste, 1t. pepper, 2T. vinegar, 1/2T. sesame oil

Procedures：

1. Cook the lean pork with 6C. water for 20 minutes. Remove the pork, cut into strings when cool. Shred the bean curd, chicken blood, black fungus (soaked in cold water for 1/4 hour), and bamboo shoot (cooked) into strings 5~6cm long. Beat the egg.
2. Boil the soup (remaining from cooked pork). Add all the ingredients except the egg. Season with salt and soy sauce. Bring to a boil, thicken with cornstarch paste. Turn to low heat, pour the egg into soup.
3. Place pepper, sesame oil, and vinegar in a soup bowl. Add the soup and sprinkle green onion on top, serve.

連鍋湯
Sliced Pork Soup, Sze - chuan Style

材料：
豬夾心肉（或後腿肉）6兩、蔥2支、薑3片、花椒粒1茶匙、白蘿蔔1個

調味料：
鹽1/2茶匙

沾料：醬油1大匙、辣豆瓣醬1茶匙、醋、辣油各1茶匙、麻油1/2茶匙、蔥屑1/2大匙

做法：
1. 將豬肉整塊加開水6杯及花椒粒、蔥段、薑片，以小火煮半小時。
2. 撈出豬肉、待稍冷後，切成4公分長方大薄片，再重新放到小鍋中，並加入切成薄片（5公分長、1.5公分寬）之白蘿蔔，繼續用小火再煮20分鐘。
3. 夾出蔥、薑及花椒粒，加入鹽調味後，整鍋端到餐桌上食用（每人一份調妥之沾料，用來沾食鍋中之肉片及白蘿蔔片）。

ingredients：
240g. pork (leg part), 2 stalks green onion, 3 slices ginger, 1t. brown peppercorn, 1 radish

Seasonings：
1/2 t. salt

Dipping sauce： 1T. soy sauce, 1t. hot bean paste, 1t. vinegar, 1/2t. sesame oil, 1/2T. chopped green onion

Procedures：
1. Boil the whole piece of pork with 6C. water (add green onion, ginger, and brown peppercorn in water) for 1/2 hour.
2. Remove the pork and slice into very thin pieces (about 4cm wide) when it cools. Return the pork to the soup. Cut radish into 0.6cm thin slices (5cm long × 1.5cm wide), also add to the soup. Simmer together for 20 minutes.
3. Remove green onion, ginger, and brown peppercorn. Season with salt. Serve with the dipping sauce (the sauce is for dipping the pork and radish).

蝦丸湯
Shrimp Ball Soup

材料：

蝦仁12兩、韭黃丁少許、蔥2支、薑5片、蛋白1個、太白粉3大匙、清湯6杯

調味料：

(1) 鹽1/2茶匙、酒1大匙
(2) 鹽1茶匙、胡椒粉少許、麻油少許

做法：

1. 蝦仁用鹽抓洗後，用水沖淨、瀝乾。全部放在砧板上，用刀面壓碎（壓二次）再仔細用刀斬剁，使成極細的蝦泥狀，盛入大碗中。（也可以放入食物調理機中打成泥。）
2. 用一只小碗裝3大匙水，放下拍碎之蔥、薑，浸泡10分鐘，成為蔥薑水。蛋白在小碗中打散。
3. 蝦泥中加入鹽、酒，朝同一方向攪拌，並將蔥薑水陸續加入（一面加一面攪，至蝦泥完全吸收），將打散之蛋白亦加入，攪拌至蝦泥富有黏性（約需5分鐘），放下太白粉仔細拌勻即可。
4. 在鍋中將清湯煮滾後改小火，將蝦泥抓在左手中，撥弄大拇指捏擠出圓形蝦球，右手拿沾過冷水的湯匙，取下蝦球投入清湯中，待全部做完後，將火稍開大、煮2分鐘，至蝦丸全部浮起，便可加鹽調味。熄火後撒下韭黃段、胡椒粉及麻油便可起鍋盛入大碗。

Ingredients:

450g. peeled shrimp, 2T. diced white leek, 2 stalks green onion, 5 slices ginger, 2T. egg white, 3T. cornstarch, 6C. soup stock

Seasonings:

(1) 1/2t. salt, 1T. wine
(2) 1t. salt, pepper, sesame oil

Procedures:

1. Clean the shrimp with salt. Rinse and pat dry. Smash the shrimp, then pound it with the back of a clever until it is finely chopped (or you may use food processor to make it into paste). Put in a large bowl.
2. Crush the green onions and ginger, soak with 3T. water for 10 minutes. Beat the egg white.
3. Add salt and wine to the shrimp. Stir in one direction. Add green onion water little by little while stirring. Add the egg white and continue to stir until the shrimp paste is very sticky (about 5 minutes). Add cornstarch, mix well.
4. Bring the soup stock to a boil, reduce to low heat. Place 1T. shrimp mixture in the left hand, shaping it into a ball about walnut size. Add the ball to the soup with a wet spoon. Make all the shrimp balls. Boil over medium heat for 2 minutes. Season with salt after all the shrimp balls are floating. Turn off the heat, sprinkle with white leeks, pepper and sesame oil. Remove to a large bowl.

湯品

136

鳳梨苦瓜雞
Chicken Soup with Pineapple

材料：
土雞或半土雞1/2隻、苦瓜1條、醃鳳梨1杯、蔥2支、薑片4片

調味料：
酒1大匙、胡椒粉少許

做法：
1. 雞剁成小塊，用滾水川燙一下，撈出洗淨。苦瓜剖開去籽，切成塊狀。
2. 湯鍋中煮滾8杯水，放下雞塊和蔥、薑、酒，煮滾後改小火，燉煮約20分鐘。
3. 將醃鳳梨連汁和苦瓜一起加入湯中，再以小火煮約30~40分鐘至喜愛的軟爛度，嚐過味道，看是否需要加鹽調味，並撒下胡椒粉即可。

Ingredients：
1/2 chicken, 1 bitter gourd, 1C. marinade salty pineapple (in jar), 2stalks green onion, 4 slice ginger

Seasonings：
1T. wine, pepper

Procedures：
1. Cut the chicken into pieces, boil for 1 minute, drain and rinse. Halve the bitter gourd, remove seeds, cut into pieces.
2. Bring 8 cups of water to a boil, add chicken, green onion, ginger, and wine. Cook over high heat, reduce to low heat after it boils. Simmer for 20 minutes.
3. Add pineapple (with the juice) and the bitter gourd, simmer for another 30~40 minutes until tender enough. Taste it first, adjust the taste with salt and pepper.

* 燉雞湯時火候要小，但也不能太小，要保持湯的滾動，才能將雞的鮮味燉出來。苦瓜雞湯中還可以加放丁香魚，以增鮮味。
* **Cook over low heat while simmer the chicken soup.**
* **You may add some small fish in soup to make it more delicious.**

香菇肉羹
Meat Potage

材料：
瘦肉6兩、魚漿6兩、香菇4朵、白菜梗絲1杯、胡蘿蔔絲1/2杯、開水6杯

調味料：
(1) 醬油1/2大匙、太白粉1大匙、水1大匙
(2) 醬油1大匙、鹽1茶匙、太白粉水3大匙
(3) 炸紅蔥頭屑、香菜屑、大蒜泥、胡椒粉、麻油各適量

做法：
1. 選用前腿部分之瘦肉，切成3公分長的粗條狀，用調味料（1）拌勻，醃20分鐘後，加入魚漿拌合。
2. 鍋中燒滾6杯水，將白菜梗絲、香菇絲（泡軟切絲）及胡蘿蔔絲加入，煮至白菜變軟後，將第一項肉料一條條投入鍋中，用小火煮熟（約3分鐘），放醬油、鹽調味，淋下太白粉水勾芡成糊狀。
3. 盛在大湯碗中，撒下適量的調味料（3）便可上桌。

＊夏季時可用綠竹筍或麻筍代替白菜。

＊**You may use bamboo shoot instead of cabbage in the summer times.**

Ingredients：
240g. lean pork, 240g. minced fish paste, 4 black mushrooms, 1C. shredded Chinese cabbage, 1/2C. shredded carrot, 6C. boiling water

Seasonings：
(1) 1/2T. soy sauce, 1T. cornstarch, 1T. water
(2) 1T. soy sauce, 1t. salt, 3T. cornstarch paste
(3) fried red shallot, chopped coriander, mashed garlic, pepper, sesame oil

Procedures：
1. Cut the pork into strips 3cm long × 0.7cm wide. Soak with seasonings (1) for 20 minutes. Mix with minced fish paste.
2. Boil the 6C. water, add shredded Chinese cabbage, carrots, and black mushrooms (soaked in water for about 20 minutes, then shredded it). Cook for about 10 minutes until the Chinese cabbage is soft. Add pork strips to the soup piece by piece. Cook over low heat for 3 minutes. Season with soy sauce and salt. Thicken with cornstarch paste.
3. Remove to a large serving bowl. Sprinkle with seasonings(3). Serve.

冬菇燉雞湯
Chicken & Black Mushroom Soup

材料：
半土雞1/2隻或雞腿2支、小香菇8朵、薑2片

調味料：
酒1大匙、鹽2茶匙、開水6杯

做法：

1. 將雞連骨斬剁成3公分四方大小，全部用開水燙1分鐘。撈出後，將有血塊處摘淨、沖洗清爽，裝入蒸碗或盅內。
2. 香菇用冷水泡軟，剪下菇蒂後放入雞內，並加入薑片，注滿開水，淋下酒即移到蒸籠或電鍋內，用大火蒸1小時半至2小時。
3. 撒下鹽調味後，整碗（盅）端到桌上趁熱分食。

＊ 此湯也可只用雞腳或雞翅膀蒸。

Ingredients:
1/2 chicken, 8 pieces black mushroom, 2 slices ginger

Seasonings:
1T. wine, 2t. salt, 6C. boiling water

Procedures:

1. Cut the chicken into 3cm pieces. Boil for 1 minute. Drain and rinse the chicken. Place in a soup bowl.
2. Soak the black mushrooms in cold water for 30 minutes. Cut off the stems. Place the black mushrooms and chicken to the soup bowl. Add ginger, wine, and boiling water. Steam for 1 1/2~2 hours.
3. Season with salt. Remove the bowl from the steamer and serve hot.

＊ You may also use chicken legs or chicken wings to make this soup.

湯品

排骨蔬菜湯
Sparerib & Vegetable Soup

材料：
小排骨1/2斤、蔥2支、高麗菜1/2斤、洋蔥1個、胡蘿蔔1支、番茄3個

調味料：
鹽2茶匙、胡椒粉隨意

做法：
1. 小排骨切成3公分長，洗淨後，在3杯開水中燙20秒鐘，撈出洗淨。再投入另外6杯的開水中，加蔥2支同煮約半小時。
2. 高麗菜洗淨、切成半個手掌大小；洋蔥切1.5公分寬條；胡蘿蔔切滾刀塊；番茄用開水燙過、剝皮後，每個切為6塊。
3. 炒鍋內燒熱3大匙油，放入洋蔥，用小火慢慢炒軟，至洋蔥香氣透出。
4. 加入番茄再炒片刻，再繼續加入高麗菜及胡蘿蔔同炒，炒至高麗菜已軟，即注入第一項之排骨湯同煮，約20分鐘，至胡蘿蔔夠爛為止，加鹽調味，便可裝大碗中。

Ingredients：
300g. spareribs, 2 stalks green onion, 300g. cabbage, 1 onion, 1 carrot, 3 tomatoes

Seasonings：
2t. salt, black pepper

Procedures：
1. Cut the spareribs into 3cm pieces. Boil in 3C. water for 20 seconds. Remove and rinse. Cook with another 6C. boiling water, bring to a boil, simmer for 1/2 hour (add 2 green onions).
2. Cut the cabbage into pieces 6cm long；slice the onion 1.5cm wide. Cut carrots into 1cm cubes. Peel tomatoes and cut into 6 pieces per tomato.
3. Heat 3T. oil to stir-fry onion over low heat until the onion becomes soft and fragrant.
4. Add tomatoes, stir-fry again. Add cabbage and carrot, stir-fry until the cabbage is soft. Add the spareribs and soup. Simmer for about 20 minutes, until the carrots are soft. Season with salt. Remove to a soup bowl and serve.

＊不用排骨湯時，用約5大匙油炒香蔬菜亦可，同時還可以加入馬鈴薯、洋菇丁同煮。

＊If you do not use the soup stock, you may use about 5T. oilto stir-fry the vegetables. Any vegetable may be used in this soup.

蟹肉豆腐羹
Crab Meat Potage

材料：
蟹腿肉4兩、營養豆腐1盒、蔥2支、薑3片、豆腐衣2張、青蒜絲少許、清湯6杯

調味料：
（1）鹽¼茶匙、太白粉½大匙、酒1茶匙
（2）酒1大匙、醬油1大匙、鹽1茶匙、太白粉4大匙、水6大匙、胡椒粉酌量

做法：
1. 蟹肉化凍後一條條的分開，略沖一下，用調味料（1）拌勻，冷藏30分鐘。臨要下鍋之前，用滾水川燙10秒，取出泡冷水中。
2. 炒鍋中用2大匙油將蔥段及薑片煎黃，淋下酒爆香後，加入清湯煮滾。將切成1.5公分四方丁之營養豆腐加入，並用醬油、鹽調味，再煮滾。
3. 加入撕成小片之豆腐衣和蟹腿肉，用調水之太白粉勾芡，裝在大碗中。撒下青蒜絲及胡椒粉便可上桌（也可將蛋汁淋下，代替撕成小片之豆腐衣）。

Ingredients：
150g. crab leg, 1 pack soft bean curd, 2 stalks green onion, 3 slices ginger, 2 pieces dried soy bean sheets, 1T. shredded green garlic, 6C. soup stock

Seasonings：
(1) ¼t. salt, ½T. cornstarch, 1t. wine
(2) 1T. wine, 1T. soy sauce, 1t. salt, 4T. cornstarch, 6T. water, pepper

Procedures：
1. Rinse the crab legs quickly after it defrost. Separate each piece. Mix with seasonings (1) for 30 minutes. Blanch for 10 seconds before cook it. Soak in cold water.
2. Stir-fry the green onion and ginger with 3 T. oil. Sprinkle wine in. Add soup stock and bring to a boil. Add bean curd cubes, season with soy sauce and salt. Boil it again.
3. Add crab legs, and dried soy bean sheets (torn into small pieces). Thicken with cornstarch paste. Remove to a bowl. Sprinkle with green garlic and pepper. Serve.(you may pour the beaten egg into soup instead of soy bean sheets)

蘿蔔絲蛤蜊湯
Clams & Radish Soup

材料：
蛤蜊15粒、白蘿蔔1/2斤、嫩薑絲1/4杯、清湯或水6杯、香菜少許

調味料：
鹽2/3茶匙、白胡椒粉少許

做法：

1. 蛤蜊要浸泡在薄鹽水中吐沙，約2~3小時後，洗淨備用。
2. 白蘿蔔削去皮後，直切成細絲（約5~6公分長），在滾水中燙1分鐘撈出，用冷水沖涼。
3. 鍋中燒滾清湯後，放下蘿蔔絲，以小火煮至蘿蔔絲夠軟而透明時，放下嫩薑絲和蛤蜊，大火煮至蛤蜊均已開口便熄火，加鹽調味，撒下香菜和白胡椒粉即可裝碗上桌。

＊江浙菜中有蘿蔔絲鯽魚湯是將鯽魚整條洗淨後與蘿蔔絲同煮，至湯汁白濃爲止，味極鮮美而營養。

Ingredients：
15 clams, 300g. radish, 1/4C. shredded young ginger, 6C. soup stock or water, coriander

Seasonings：
2/3t. salt, white pepper

Procedures：

1. Soak clams with salty water (2 cups of water and 1/2t. salt) for 2~3 hours, rinse.
2. Peel and shred the radish into strips about 5~6cm long. Boil for 1 minute. Remove and soak in cold water.
3. Boil 6C. soup stock. Add radish, simmer until it becomes soft. Add clams and ginger. Cook over high heat until the clams have opened. Season with salt, sprinkle coriander and pepper. Remove to a soup bowl and serve.

＊ You may cook gold carp with radish, also very delicious.

附錄

POSTSCRIPT

145 ... 冰糖燕窩

146 ... 三絲魚翅
　　　　蠔油扒鮑魚

147 ... 蔥燒海參
　　　　紹子蹄筋

148 ... 金鉤魷魚絲
　　　　魚香肉絲

149 ... 酸辣海參
　　　　宮保蝦仁

150 ... 麻辣雞丁
　　　　古老肉

151 ... 五味九孔
　　　　涼拌海蜇

152 ... 乾煎鯧魚
　　　　各式炸排骨

153 ... 沙茶炒午肉
　　　　火爆鮮魷捲

烹飪入門示範料理

觀賞DVD，邊看邊學
跟著傅培梅老師
　　一起進入美食天地

154 ... 醋溜明蝦片
　　　　炸烹蝦仁

155 ... 燙青菜兩式
　　　　川蝦丸湯

156 ... 羅宋湯
　　　　各式滷味

157 ... 香菇肉羹
　　　　紅燒子排

158 ... 清蒸鮮魚
　　　　佛跳牆

159 ... 鮪魚香菇盒
　　　　燻雞腿

冰糖燕窩

> 材料：

燕窩 5錢、紅棗 20粒、冰糖 2湯匙、水 4杯

> 做法：

① 紅棗洗淨，是否要泡水，視燕窩之軟度而定，如燕窩已發得很軟，只需再蒸20分鐘，則紅棗要先泡水1～2小時，至紅棗也漲軟，再放入燕窩中同蒸。如果燕窩不夠軟，還要再蒸久一點，則紅棗只要洗淨便可加入同蒸。

② 乾燕窩發泡好後，用小篩網將燕窩瀝出，放入蒸碗中，加入冰糖、紅棗和水一起上鍋蒸1小時，見燕窩已夠柔軟，便可端出分食之。

> 註：燕窩本身無味，所以藉紅棗的香氣和冰糖的清甜來搭配。同樣做法還可以用白木耳來做"冰糖銀耳"、用蓮子來做"冰糖蓮子"。燕窩可補氣、潤肺、養顏是很滋補的保養品。

三絲魚翅

> 材料：
散翅 4兩、雞胸 半個、香菇 4朵、筍 1個、熟火腿絲 1湯匙、高湯 8杯、香菜 少許

> 醃雞料：
鹽 1/6茶匙、太白粉 1茶匙、水 1湯匙

> 調味料：
醬油 1湯匙、鹽 酌量、濕太白粉 1 1/2湯匙

> 做法：
① 散翅發好後，用高湯2杯煨煮至軟，用小篩網瀝出。
② 雞胸去骨去皮，肉切絲，用醃雞料拌勻，醃半小時以上，用七分熱油過油至熟。
③ 香菇泡軟切絲。筍去殼煮熟，切成細絲，約有1杯的份量。
④ 高湯6杯煮滾後加入香菇絲及筍絲，小火煮滾片刻。放下雞絲及魚翅，先加醬油調勻成茶色（可酌量多加醬油），再加鹽補充鹹味，用濕太白粉勾芡後撒下火腿絲，便可倒入大湯碗中，綴以少許香菜即可上桌。

> 註：這道散翅的湯菜，可以將湯的份量減少，做成一道湯少料多的燴菜。魚翅羹亦可加入切絲之魚皮、白菜梗絲和金菇絲，但魚翅份量不宜太少。

蠔油扒鮑魚

> 材料：
發好之小鮑魚 10粒、西洋生菜 半球、蔥 2支薑 2片、高湯 1杯

> 調味料：
醬油 1湯匙、糖 1茶匙、蠔油 1湯匙
濕太白粉 酌量、熱油 1湯匙

> 做法：
① 用2湯匙油煎香蔥段、薑片，注入醬油、糖和高湯，淋到發好之鮑魚中（原鮑魚湯加入），再煨至夠軟，湯汁還餘1杯半左右，用濕太白粉勾芡，加入蠔油調味，淋下熱油調勻。
② 西生菜洗淨，切成大片或寬條。滾水中加少許油（約1茶匙），放下西洋生菜，不必等水再滾，一燙軟即可撈出，瀝乾後墊在盤中間，將(1)項中之鮑魚連汁盛在生菜上便可上桌。

> 註：如用罐頭的鮑魚，可直接切片或橫刀片成大片來做這道菜，將高湯煮滾後再放下鮑片，迅速勾芡，並加蠔油調味即可。
罐頭鮑魚用途很多，可做冷盤，切絲來炒或扒、燴、燒、蒸均可。

蔥燒海參

> **材料：**
> 海參 5條、蔥 6支、薑 3片、花椒粒 1茶匙

> **調味料：**
> 酒 1湯匙、醬油 2湯匙、糖 1茶匙、清湯 3/4杯、濕太白粉 1湯匙

> **做法：**
>
> ① 海參放在湯鍋中出水，加冷水4杯，蔥1支、薑1片和酒半湯匙，煮滾後改小火，煮5～10分鐘，視海參軟硬程度而定，取出沖冷水，可以整條來燒或斜刀片切成大片再燒。
>
> ② 鍋中用2湯匙油小火爆香花椒粒，撈棄花椒粒，放下蔥段、薑片煎香，再落海參入鍋，大火爆炒，淋下酒及高湯，用醬油和糖調味，大火燒煮3分鐘，用濕太白粉勾芡，便可裝盤。

> **註：** 海參無論是自己發的或是買現成發好的，都要經過出水的步驟，以去腥味，出水時間長短，視海參之軟硬度而定，但有時不易控制相同軟度，可將已軟的先撈出，未軟的多煮一會兒。一定記得冷水下鍋煮才能去腥。
>
> 海參本身無味，所以多用紅燒或燴等口味較重的燒法來烹調，常和蹄筋、蹄花或小排骨雞翅塊來燒。

紹子蹄筋

> **材料：**
> 蹄筋 12兩、絞肉 1湯匙、芹菜屑 2湯匙、蔥花 1湯匙

> **調味料：**
> 醬油 2湯匙、酒 少許、高湯 1杯、濕太白粉 酌量
> 麻油 1茶匙、胡椒粉 少許

> **做法：**
> 做法：
>
> ① 蹄筋發好後或買已發好的，都要先出水煮過，鍋中加水、蔥、薑和酒，小火煮約10分鐘（時間長短可視蹄筋軟硬而增減），以除腥味，撈出沖涼後，切為兩段。
>
> ② 用2湯匙油先爆香絞肉及蔥花，再放下蹄筋大火炒一下，淋下醬油及酒，再加水或高湯，小火燜煮一下（約3分鐘），用少許濕太白粉勾芡，淋下麻油，灑下芹菜屑和胡椒粉，便可裝盤。

> **註：** 蹄筋也常放在砂鍋中或做成湯菜或燴菜，也可以用來紅燒海參，因其本身無味，所以也常借助蟹肉、蝦子、冬菇、干貝等有鮮香味的材料來搭配提味。

147

金鉤魷魚絲

> 材料：

乾魷魚 1條、鹼塊 1/4塊（一寸四方）、
或鹼粉 1湯匙、開水 2杯、瘦豬肉 3兩、
香菇 3朵、筍 1支、韭黃 2兩、紅辣椒 1支

> 調味料：

酒 半湯匙、淡色醬油 2湯匙、鹽 1/4茶匙
醋 半湯匙、麻油 1茶匙

> 做法：

1. 乾魷魚從尾部捲起，用刀切成絲或逆絲剪成細絲，放在大碗中，加鹼塊及滾水（滾水要蓋過魷魚3公分以上），拌合後泡30分鐘左右，用手指試一下魷魚是否夠軟，以清水洗淨，瀝乾待用。
2. 豬肉切絲，香菇泡軟切絲，筍煮熟切絲，韭黃洗淨切段，紅辣椒去籽切絲。
3. 將3湯匙油燒熱後放下魷魚絲，大火炒5秒鐘，見魷魚絲已捲曲，瀝出，油倒掉。
4. 另用2湯匙油炒肉絲、香菇絲、紅辣椒絲及筍絲，炒勻後倒下魷魚絲，淋酒並以醬油和鹽調味，沿鍋邊淋下醋，拌炒均勻，撒下韭黃關火，滴下麻油拌合即可。

魚香肉絲

> 材料：

瘦豬肉 半斤、荸薺 6個（或筍1支）、乾木耳 2湯匙
薑屑 2茶匙、蒜屑 1茶匙

> 醃肉料：

醬油 1湯匙、太白粉 1湯匙、水 2湯匙

> 綜合調味料：

蔥屑 1湯匙、醬油 1湯匙、醋和酒 各1/2湯匙
辣豆瓣醬 1又1/2湯匙、糖 2茶匙、鹽 1/4茶匙
水 1湯匙、太白粉和麻油各 1茶匙、花椒粉 1/4茶匙

> 做法：

1. 豬肉切絲後，用醃肉料拌醃15分鐘以上。木耳泡軟摘根，切成絲，荸薺去皮切絲，小碗中調好綜合調味料。
2. 將2杯油燒至七分熱，倒下肉絲過油，肉絲變色熟後即瀝出。
3. 另用2湯匙油爆香薑、蒜屑，放下木耳及荸薺絲同炒，再加入肉絲拌炒數下，淋下綜合調味料拌勻，熱透即可裝盤。

酸辣海參

> 材料：
海參 3條、絞肉 2湯匙、蔥花 1湯匙、薑末 1茶匙、芹菜屑 1湯匙

> 出水料：
蔥 1支、薑 2片、酒 1湯匙、冷水 3杯

> 調味料：
辣豆瓣醬 1湯匙、酒 1/2湯匙、醬油 1湯匙、鹽 1/4茶匙、高湯 2/3杯、濕太白粉 1湯匙、醋 1湯匙、麻油 1茶匙、胡椒粉 少許

> 做法：
1. 海參整條放在湯鍋中，加出水料，煮滾後改小火，煮5～10分鐘，視海參軟硬度而定，不要煮的太軟爛，撈出海參沖涼後，切成約3寸長粗絲。
2. 鍋中用2湯匙油炒散絞肉後，放下蔥花、薑末及辣豆瓣醬，炒至有香氣透出，淋下酒、醬油、鹽及高湯，並加入海參，中火煮3分鐘，用濕太白粉勾芡，關火後加入醋及麻油、胡椒粉拌勻，最後撒下芹菜屑，便可裝盤。

宮保蝦仁

> 材料：
大型海蝦或小草蝦 1斤、乾辣椒 8支、花椒粒 1茶匙、薑屑 1茶匙

> 醃蝦料：
鹽 1/2茶匙、太白粉 1/2湯匙、蛋白 半個

> 綜合調味料：
深色醬油 1湯匙、糖 1/2湯匙、酒 1茶匙、醋 1茶匙、麻油 1/2茶匙、太白粉 1茶匙

> 做法：
1. 蝦剝殼，如較大型的蝦可留尾殼，並將背上剖劃一刀，使蝦仁熟後可以捲成蝦球狀。用鹽抓洗乾淨，擦乾水份，再用醃蝦料拌醃30分鐘，最好放入冰箱中冰過。
2. 乾辣椒用濕紙巾擦乾淨，切成1寸長段。小碗中將綜合調味料調勻備用。
3. 鍋中將2杯油燒至8分熱，放下蝦仁過油，待蝦仁變色即可撈出，瀝淨油。
4. 用1湯匙油，小火將花椒粒炸香後撈棄，再放下乾辣椒段，小火炸至黑，放下蝦仁，同時淋下綜合調味料，大火拌炒均勻便可關火，裝盤。

麻辣雞丁

> 材料：
> 雞肉 半斤、青椒（小）1個、紅辣椒 2支、蔥 2支、薑片 6片

> 醃雞料：
> 醬油 1湯匙、太白粉 1湯匙、水 1湯匙

> 綜合調味料：
> 醬油 1湯匙、酒 1/2湯匙、醋 1茶匙、糖 1茶匙、辣豆瓣醬 1湯匙、鹽 1/4茶匙、
> 花椒粉 1/4茶匙、太白粉 1/2茶匙

> 做法：
> ① 可選購雞胸或雞腿部份，去骨後連皮切成1寸大小，用醃雞料拌勻醃30分鐘。
> ② 青椒、紅椒分別去籽切小片，蔥切段，小碗中調好綜合調味料備用。
> ③ 鍋子先燒熱，再放下1杯油，待油燒至8分熱時，放下雞丁，大火過油至9分熟，撈出瀝乾油。
> ④ 另用2湯匙油爆香蔥段和薑片，放下雞丁和青、紅椒片，大火拌炒數下，淋下綜合調味料，炒勻後即可盛出。

咕咾肉

> 材料：
> 豬肉（大排肉或梅花肉）半斤、青椒（小）1個、洋蔥 半個、罐頭鳳梨 3片、太白粉 半杯

> 醃肉料：
> 淡色醬油 1/2湯匙、太白粉 1湯匙、水 1湯匙、蛋黃 1個

> 綜合調味料：
> 米醋 3湯匙、糖 4湯匙、水 5湯匙、蕃茄醬 4湯匙、鹽 1/2茶匙、太白粉 1湯匙、麻油 1茶匙

> 做法：
> ① 豬肉用刀背敲鬆，切成1寸四方之小塊。碗中拌勻醃肉料，放入肉塊拌勻，醃半小時以上。
> ② 青椒去籽子和洋蔥均切成1寸四方，鳳梨也切小塊。
> ③ 碗中調好綜合調味料。
> ④ 炸之前用乾太白粉沾裹肉塊。將3杯油燒至八分熱，放入肉塊到油中，小火慢炸。約2分鐘後撈出，將油再燒熱，重新用大火再炸20秒至肉塊黃且酥脆即撈出。
> ⑤ 另用2湯匙油，大火炒香洋蔥，放下青椒及鳳梨，倒下綜合調味料煮滾，關火後倒下肉塊拌合，儘速裝盤。

五味九孔

> 材料：
>
> 九孔 12粒、酒 1/2湯匙
>
> 五味汁：
>
> 醬油膏 1湯匙、蕃茄醬 1/2湯匙（或甜辣醬）、糖 1/2湯匙、醋 1/2茶匙、大蒜泥 1茶匙、紅辣椒屑 1/2茶匙、蔥屑 1/2湯匙、麻油 少許

> 做法：
>
> ❶ 九孔最好選購活的，肉質才會鮮嫩，刷洗乾淨（肉下面的腸泥可以除去，也可依個人喜好而保留），排入盤中，分別淋上少許酒，連盤放入蒸籠中（水已先煮滾），大火蒸4～5分鐘（視九孔大小而定），蒸好後排在盤中。
>
> ❷ 小碗中調好五味汁，淋在九孔上即可上桌。

> 說明：五味汁是最近幾年才流行的口味，以台菜中應用最廣，多用以沾食燙或煮或蒸的海鮮。新鮮海鮮肉質鮮嫩，以清蒸或白灼（燙）最能保持其原味，所以五味汁中無論加蒜泥或薑汁或剁碎的紅辣椒都不能下的很重，五味要均勻調和，不能奪味。

涼拌海蜇

> 材料：
>
> 海蜇皮 1張（約2兩）、蝦米 2湯匙、大白菜絲 2杯、胡蘿蔔絲 1/2杯、香菜段 1/3杯

> 調味料：
>
> 醬油 2湯匙、醋 1湯匙、麻油 2湯匙、蒜泥 1茶匙

> 做法：
>
> ❶ 海蜇用水漂洗一下，沖除鹽粒後，捲成筒狀，切成細絲。用冷水泡2～3小時。煮滾8杯水，加入冷水1杯，放下海蜇絲燙3秒鐘，立刻撈出沖冷水，並浸在冷水中再泡2～3小時，至海蜇發漲開來為止。
>
> ❷ 蝦米泡軟，撿除頭和腳和大白菜絲、胡蘿蔔絲及香菜都放在大碗中，並加入海蜇絲（可改刀切成4寸長）。
>
> ❸ 小碗中調好三合油調味料，倒入(2)項材料中，仔細拌勻，剛拌時不夠入味，可以放置半小時左右再吃。

乾煎鯧魚

> 材料：

鯧魚 1條（約1斤）、蔥 2支、薑 2片、鹽 1茶匙、酒 1湯匙、油 半杯

> 做法：

1. 蔥切段與薑片一起拍碎，放在盤中與酒拌合，抓一抓，將蔥薑的汁擠出來。魚洗淨擦乾，切割刀口後用鹽抹勻，再將蔥薑汁也抹在魚肉上，醃20分鐘以上。
2. 鍋子先燒熱，加入油再燒熱，放下魚大火煎半分鐘，改小火慢慢煎。魚比較大時，可以轉動鍋子，使魚頭、尾各部份均煎到，煎5分鐘後便可翻一面，翻面後火可以增強一點，再約3分鐘把火再改大一點，把魚皮煎黃。如喜愛焦黃酥脆的，可以再翻面用大火再煎一下。撈出瀝乾油裝盤，洒上黑胡椒粉或附花椒鹽等沾料油食之。

> 說明：還要記住的就是不要太早去翻動魚，魚貼在鍋子的一面還沒煎硬成型，魚肉半生不熟時，最容易破了，魚肉越厚的魚，煎的時候，火要越小，慢慢煎熟，再改大火煎酥脆。

各式炸排骨

> 材料：

大排骨 2片、蕃薯粉 2/3杯

> 調味料：

大蒜 2粒、醬油 2湯匙、酒、糖 各1茶匙、胡椒粉 少許

> 做法：

1. 大排骨用刀面拍得大些，再用刀背敲一敲，並將白筋切斷，以免熟後會縮。
2. 大蒜拍一下放入碗中，加入所有調味料調勻，放下排骨醃10分鐘以上，如果醃的時間長，可減少醬油的份量。
3. 排骨臨炸前沾上蕃薯粉，沾好後可放3～5分鐘，使蕃薯粉附著牢一點，投入8分熱油中，先大火炸一下，再改小火炸，再炸約1分鐘便熟了，撈出排骨把油瀝乾。

另外介紹清炸排骨（醃好直接炸），酥炸排骨（醃料中加麵粉、太白粉和水調成的糊，醃過再炸，外層有一層酥酥的外皮）和西炸排骨三種不同方式炸出來的排骨，以供參考。

沙茶炒牛肉

> 材料：
牛肉 12兩、洋蔥（中型）1個、薑絲 酌量

> 醃料：
醬油 1湯匙、太白粉、水 各1湯匙、
嫩精 少許（可免）

> 調味料：
沙茶醬 1又1/2湯匙、水 1/2湯匙、醬油 1湯匙、麻油少許

> 做法：
1. 牛肉逆紋切絲，大碗中先將醃肉料調勻，放下牛肉仔細拌勻，醃30分鐘，最好放入冰箱中。
2. 洋蔥切塊或絲均可，用油炒軟，加鹽1/4匙調味，盛入盤中墊底。沙茶醬、醬油、水和麻油在小碗中調勻。
3. 油2杯燒至7分熟，放下牛肉絲，將牛肉絲快速攪散，至8分熟即撈出，油倒掉，僅留1湯匙左右。
4. 薑絲爆香，再將牛肉絲放回鍋中，並將沙茶醬調味料倒入，大火拌炒均勻，關火淋少許熱油，便可盛到洋蔥上。

火爆鮮魷捲

> 材料：
中型鮮魷 2條、青椒 1個、紅辣椒 1支、蔥 2支、薑片 10小片

> 調味料：
淡色醬油 1/2湯匙、酒 1湯匙、鹽 1/2茶匙、醋、胡椒粉、麻油 各少許

> 做法：
1. 鮮魷撕去外層之薄膜，在內部切交叉刀紋，再分割成菱角塊，用半鍋滾水燙至捲起，立即撈出。
2. 蔥切斜段，青、紅椒去籽，分別切菱角片。
3. 燒熱2湯匙油，爆香蔥段、薑片，再放下青、紅椒和鮮魷捲，淋下調味料（調勻在小碗中），大火拌炒數下即可盛出。

醋溜明蝦片

> 材料：
明蝦 5隻、木耳（泡好） 1杯、胡蘿蔔 半小支、毛豆 1湯匙、大蒜片 1湯匙、太白粉 1/2杯

> 醃蝦料：
鹽 1/4茶匙、蛋白 半個、太白粉 1/2湯匙

> 調味料：
白醋 3湯匙、糖 3湯匙、水 6湯匙、鹽 1/2茶匙、太白粉 1/2湯匙、麻油 少許

> 做法：
1. 明蝦剝去外殼（留下尾殼），再片開成2片，每片都帶一截尾殼，用醃蝦料拌醃30分鐘，用乾太白粉沾裹。
2. 胡蘿蔔煮軟切片，毛豆燙熟，木耳泡好，撕成小片。
3. 燒熱4杯油後，放下明蝦片炸至熟且酥脆，撈出。另用2湯匙油炒香大蒜片，再放入木耳及胡蘿蔔同炒，倒下綜合調味料煮滾，放下毛豆及蝦片迅速一拌，馬上盛入盤中。

炸烹蝦仁

> 材料：
蝦仁 5兩、蔥花 1湯匙、蒜末 1茶匙

> 醃蝦料：
鹽 1/4茶匙、酒、太白粉 各1茶匙、蛋白 半個

> 蛋麵糊：
蛋 1個、麵粉 3湯匙、水 酌量

> 調味料：
酒、醋 各1茶匙、鹽 1/4茶匙、麻油 1/2茶匙

> 做法：
1. 蝦仁抽去腸砂，用鹽抓洗，沖乾淨後，擦乾水份，用醃蝦料醃10分鐘。
2. 蛋麵糊調好，放入蝦仁拌上蛋麵糊，投入油中炸至黃且脆（可以炸兩次）。
3. 油倒出，將大蒜末放入爆香，再放蔥花及蝦仁下鍋，淋下調味料，很快速一拌即可關火，略翻拌兩三下即可。

燙青菜兩式

> 材料：
芥蘭菜 半斤、韭菜 6兩、柴魚片 酌量
> 調味料：
油 1/2湯匙、鹽 1茶匙、蠔油 1湯匙、
醬油膏 1湯匙
> 做法：
① 芥蘭菜洗淨，撿掉一些老梗部份，鍋中燒滾水，水中加1茶匙鹽，放下芥蘭菜燙1分鐘，撈出瀝乾水份，排列整齊，對切為兩段後放入盤中，淋上油及蠔油1湯匙。（油也可加在水中一起燙青菜）
② 韭菜也可以在滾水中燙過，用冷開水沖冷，擠乾水份，切成1寸長段，排入盤中，撒上柴魚片，附醬油膏供沾食。

川蝦丸湯

> 材料：
蝦仁 半斤、絞肥豬肉 1～2湯匙、豆苗 數支、清湯或水 6杯
> 拌蝦料：
蛋白 1個、鹽 1/2茶匙、蔥薑水 2湯匙、酒 1/2湯匙、太白粉 1湯匙
> 調味料：
鹽 1茶匙、酒 1/2茶匙
> 做法：
① 蝦仁用刀面壓碎，再用刀背剁成泥，放入碗小，加入拌蝦料，朝同一方向仔細拌勻，多加攪拌使之有黏性。
② 鍋中水煮至七分熱後，改小火，將蝦泥做成丸子狀，投入滾水中，全部做好，用小火煮至蝦丸全部浮起，加鹽及酒調味，放下豆苗，關火一拌即熟，便可全部倒入湯碗中，碗中可放白胡椒粉及麻油以增香氣。
> 說明：也可以用絞肉做成肉丸或做魚丸、花枝丸、牛肉丸來川湯。以肉片、魚片或海參片直接來川都很鮮美。

羅宋湯

> 材料：

牛肋條 1斤、包心菜 12兩、蕃茄 2個、胡蘿蔔 1支、馬鈴薯 1個、洋蔥 1個、蔥 2支、薑 1片、八角 1粒

> 調味料：

酒 1湯匙、鹽 酌量、胡椒粉 少許

> 做法：

1. 牛肉切塊燙水後，撈出，沖洗乾淨，湯鍋中另煮滾水10杯，放下牛肉及蔥、薑、八角和酒，煮滾後改小火慢慢煮約1小時（8分爛），也可以將牛肉整塊煮至8分軟時，再改刀切小塊來燒。
2. 撈棄蔥、薑及八角，加入胡蘿蔔（切塊），蕃茄（去皮切塊），馬鈴薯（切塊），洋蔥（切寬條）及包心菜（切成大片），煮滾後再改中小火，繼續煮至材料均已夠軟便可加鹽調味，並灑下少許胡椒粉。

各式滷味

> 材料：

牛腱、豬肝、豬肚、雞翅、蛋、海帶或豆乾均隨意

> 滷湯材料：

五香料（包括八角、甘草、桂皮、花椒、丁香、小茴及沙薑各酌量）、醬油 1又1/2杯、紹興酒 1/2杯、冰糖 2湯匙、鹽 1茶匙、滾水 15杯

> 做法：

滷湯：

五香料裝入白布袋中綁好（或買現成的五香包1～2包）和其他滷汁料一同放在大鍋中煮滾，改小火繼續煮20分鐘以上便成滷湯。

滷味：

A. 要滷牛腱、雞、雞翅、鴨翅、豬肝、五花肉、梅花肉或豬舌時要先在滾水中燙煮2分鐘，以除去血水，洗淨後再放入滷湯中滷，滷約七分爛，關火再燜泡在滷湯中，越大塊的材料泡的時間要越久。

B. 豬肚、豬大腸等較有異味的材料，燙過後再另用蔥薑、酒、八角加冷水煮15分鐘，再放入滷湯中去滷。

C. 海帶、豆製品（豆腐乾、素雞、蘭花乾）等要將滷湯取出一部份另外滷，以免滷湯變酸腐壞。

香菇肉羹

> 材料：
> 豬肉（夾心肉或里脊肉）6兩、魚漿 4兩、香菇 3朵、筍 1個、胡蘿蔔1小支、清湯 5杯

> 醃肉料：
> 醬油 1湯匙、酒 1茶匙、麻油、白胡椒粉 各少許

> 調味料：
> 醬油 1/2湯匙、鹽 1茶匙、濕太白粉 1湯匙

> 做法：
> 1. 將肉切成1寸長粗條，用醃肉料拌醃約半小時，用魚漿將肉條包裹住，投入滾水中川燙至熟，撈出，即為肉羹。
> 2. 香菇泡軟切絲，煮熟之胡蘿蔔及筍亦切絲。
> 3. 清湯中放下香菇絲、筍絲及胡蘿蔔絲，煮滾後放下肉羹，小火煮3分鐘，調味並勾芡，倒入湯碗中。肉羹一般在吃的時候，加入許多調味料，如蒜泥、醬油、紅蔥酥、香菜、烏酢、麻油、胡椒粉，可按個人喜愛調配。

紅燒子排

> 材料：
> 子排 1又1/2斤、蔥 5支、薑 2片、八角 1顆

> 調味料：
> 油 2湯匙、酒 1湯匙、醬油 2/3杯、冰糖 2湯匙、水 3杯

> 做法：
> 1. 子排要剁的長一點，每段約有3寸長，蔥支也切長段，也可以再多放蔥段，墊在鍋底燒。
> 2. 鍋中燒熟油2湯匙，放下蔥支及薑片爆香，再將子排放下，在油中翻炒至變色，淋酒並加醬油、冰糖、八角及水，蓋上鍋蓋，先大火煮滾，立刻改小火慢燒。
> 3. 燒約1個半小時以上，見子排已夠爛即可，此時如果湯汁還剩很多，開大火收乾湯汁，並使湯汁濃稠光亮。

清蒸鮮魚

> 材料：
>
> 新鮮鱸魚 1條（任何新鮮魚均可，約12兩）、蔥 2支、蔥絲 1杯、嫩薑絲 1/3杯、香菜 少許

> 調味料：
>
> 酒 1湯匙、蠔油 1又1/2湯匙

> 做法：
>
> ❶ 鱸魚先打理乾淨，擦乾水份，放在鋪了蔥支的盤子上，淋少許酒和薑絲，移入蒸鍋中（水要沸滾），大火蒸熟。通常12兩的魚蒸7分鐘便熟了，見魚眼已突出或用筷子試插入魚背上肉厚之處，沒有白色魚肉沾在筷子上即熟。
>
> ❷ 將魚換到另外的盤子上（天冷時可將盤子先用熱水燙一下，以免魚很快就涼了），撒下蔥絲及薑絲。鍋中燒熱2湯匙油，淋到蔥、薑絲上，再放下蠔油爆一下，也淋到蔥、薑絲上，再撒下香菜即可上桌。

佛跳牆

> 材料：
>
> 水發魚翅 半斤、海參 3條、豬腳 1個、雞腿 1支、豬肚 1/4個、蹄筋 5支、香菇 5朵、紅棗 10粒、干貝 3粒、大芋頭 1個

> 調味料：
>
> 酒 2湯匙、鹽 1茶匙、高湯 8～10杯

> 做法：
>
> ❶ 芋頭削皮切成大塊，拌過醬油後用熱油炸黃，豬腳及雞腿切小塊，也拌過醬油炸過，豬肚燙煮過切寬條，蹄筋一切為二，香菇泡軟，干貝蒸過，海參洗淨切大斜片，發好的魚翅（最好為排翅），依次放入盅內，加酒、鹽及高湯（視盅之大小來定高湯之量），用玻璃紙封好盅口。
>
> ❷ 大湯鍋中煮大半鍋水，將盅放入水中，蓋上鍋蓋，蒸燉4小時以上。上桌前蓋上盅蓋，在上桌後再揭開蓋子及封口，分裝小碗而食。

> 註：佛跳牆內所用的材料可自訂，但以名貴的放在上層，芋頭等墊底。

鮪魚香菇盒

> 材料：
> 鮪魚罐頭 1罐、新鮮香菇 10個、沙拉醬 1/2杯、洋蔥末 1湯匙、黑芝麻 1茶匙、太白粉 1湯匙、蛋黃 1個

> 調味料：
> 鹽 1/2茶匙、胡椒粉 少許

> 做法：
> 1. 將香菇之菇蒂切下，浸泡在鹽水中約10分鐘，瀝乾，在每個香菇的裡面撒下乾太白粉。
> 2. 鮪魚用叉子壓碎，放入碗中，拌入洋蔥末、沙拉醬及調味料，仔細調勻，釀入香菇裡面。將表面塗抹光滑並刷少許蛋黃汁，再裝飾數粒黑芝麻。
> 3. 烤盤上鋪一張鋁箔紙，排上香菇，移入烤箱中，用中火烤10分鐘左右至表面呈金黃便可取出排盤。

> 註：現在有許多材料可以用鋁箔紙包起來烤，如牛肉、魚肉、蝦、蛤蜊等各種海鮮類，肉嫩又保留原汁不流失。

燻雞腿

> 材料：
> 雞腿 2支、雞蛋 6個、蔥 2支、薑 2片、酒 1茶匙、鹽 1/2茶匙、糖水 少許

> 燻料：
> 紅茶 1/2杯、黃砂糖 1/2杯、麵粉 1/2杯

> 做法：
> 1. 蛋放入冷水中煮熟，剝皮。雞腿可以抹上鹽、酒和蔥、薑去蒸熟或者家中有滷湯，可以將兩種材料滷熟，取出待涼，雞皮上不要有水份。
> 2. 舊炒鍋中鋪鋁箔紙或白紙一張，上面放燻料，再架上一個燻網，網上塗油後再把雞腿和蛋放在網子上，蓋上鍋蓋，（鍋蓋如有透氣之處，要用濕布圍住鍋蓋邊緣），開大火，待冒煙後改小火慢慢燻，約15分鐘後便可取出。
> 3. 雞腿表面刷上少許糖水，再切小塊裝盤即可。

培梅家常菜

國家圖書館出版預行編目資料

培梅家常菜 / 傅培梅．程安琪著. -- 初版 --
臺北市：旗林文化，2007．08
　　面；　　公分．
中英對照　銷售20萬冊紀念版
ISBN 978-986-6881-42-8
（平裝附數位影音光碟）
1.食譜
427.11　　　　　　　　　96014429

作者/ 傅培梅・程安琪
發行人/ 程安琪
總策劃/ 程顯灝
總編輯/ 潘秉新
美術設計/ 洪瑞伯
出版者/ 旗林文化出版社有限公司
　地址/ 106台北市安和路2段213號4樓
　電話/ (02)2377-4155
　傳真/ (02)2377-4355
E-mail 信箱/ service@sanyau.com.tw

總代理/ 三友圖書有限公司
　地址/ 106台北市安和路2段213號4樓
　電話/ (02)2377-4155
　傳真/ (02)2377-4355
　網址/ http://store.pchome.com.tw/sanyau/
　E-MAIL/ sanyau@sanyau.com.tw
郵政劃撥/ 05844889　三友圖書有限公司

總經銷/ 吳氏圖書股份有限公司
　地址/ 新北市中和區中正路788-1號5樓
　電話/ (02)3234-0036
　傳真/ (02)3234-0037

新加坡/ 諾文文化事業私人有限公司
　地址/ Novum Organum Publishing House (Pte) Ltd. 20 Old Toh Tuck Road, Singapore 597655.
　電話/ 65-6462-6141
　傳真/ 65-6469-4043

馬來西亞/ 諾文文化事業私人有限公司
　地址/ Novum Organum Publishing House (M) Sdn. Bhd. No. 8, Jalan 7/118B, Desa Tun Razak, 56000 Kuala Lumpur, Malaysia
　電話/ 603-9179-6333
　傳真/ 603-9179-6060

初版/ 2007年8月
再版/ 2012年8月・一版七刷
定價/ 450元
ISBN/ 978-986-6881-42-8（平裝）

版權所有・翻印必究

書若有破損缺頁請請寄回本社更換